MANAGING INFORMATION

**Managing Universities and Colleges:
Guides to Good Practice**

Series editors:

David Warner, Principal and Chief Executive,
Swansea Institute of Higher Education

David Palfreyman, Bursar and Fellow, New College, Oxford

This series has been commissioned in order to provide systematic
analysis of the major areas of the management of colleges and universities, emphasizing good practice.

Current titles
Allan Bolton: *Managing the Academic Unit*
Judith Elkin and Derek Law (eds): *Managing Information*
John M. Gledhill: *Managing Students*
Christine Humfrey: *Managing International Students*
Colleen Liston: *Managing Quality and Standards*

Forthcoming titles include
Ann Edworthy: *Managing Stress*
David Nicol: *Managing Learning and Teaching*
Andrew Paine: *Managing Hospitality Services*
Harold Thomas: *Managing Financial Resources*
David Watson: *Managing Strategy*

MANAGING INFORMATION

Edited by
Judith Elkin and Derek Law

Open University Press
Buckingham · Philadelphia

Open University Press
Celtic Court
22 Ballmoor
Buckingham
MK18 1XW

e-mail: enquiries@openup.co.uk
world wide web: http://www.openup.co.uk

and
325 Chestnut Street
Philadelphia, PA 19106, USA

First Published 2000

A catalogue record of this book is available from the British Library

ISBN   0 335 20340 X (hb)   0 335 20339 6 (pb)

Library of Congress Cataloging-in-Publication Data
Managing information / edited by Judith Elkin and Derek Law.
      p.   cm. – (Managing universities and colleges)
   Includes bibliographical references and index.
   ISBN 0–335–20340–X. – ISBN 0–335–20339–6 (pbk.)
   1. Information resources management–Great Britain.
2. Universities and colleges–Great Britain–Administration–Data
processing. I. Elkin, Judith. II. Law, Derek G. III. Series.
LB2342.77.M25   2000
378'. 00285–dc21

99–16164
CIP

Typeset by Graphicraft Typesetters Limited, Hong Kong
Printed in Great Britain by The Cromwell Press, Trowbridge

CONTENTS

Judith Elkin

Ann Hughes

John O'Donovan

10 Information management: future perfect or past imperfect? 146

Derek Law

SERIES EDITORS' INTRODUCTION

Post-secondary educational institutions can be viewed from a variety of different perspectives. For the majority of students and staff who work in them, they are centres of learning and teaching where the participants are there by choice and consequently, by and large, work very hard. Research has always been important in some higher education institutions, but in recent years this emphasis has grown and what for many was a great pleasure and, indeed, a treat, is becoming more of a threat and an insatiable performance indicator which just has to be met. Maintaining the correct balance between quality research and learning/teaching, while the unit of resource continues to decline inexorably, is one of the key issues facing us all. Educational institutions as workplaces must be positive and not negative environments.

From another aspect, post-secondary educational institutions are clearly communities, functioning to all intents and purposes like small towns and internally requiring and providing a similar range of services, while also having very specialist needs. From yet another, they are seen as external suppliers of services to industry, commerce and the professions. These 'customers' receive, *inter alia*, a continuing flow of well-qualified fresh graduates with transferable skills, part-time and short course study opportunities through which to develop existing employees, consultancy services to solve problems and help expand business, and research and development support to create new breakthroughs.

However, educational institutions are also significant businesses in their own right. One recent study of the economic impact of higher education in Wales shows that it is of similar importance in employment terms to the steel or banking/finance sectors. Put another way, Welsh higher education institutions (HEIs) spend half a billion pounds annually and create more than 23,000 full-time equivalent jobs. And it must be remembered that there are only 13 HEIs in Wales, compared with 171 in the whole of the UK, and that these Welsh institutions are, on average, relatively small. In addition, it has recently been realized that UK higher education is a major export industry with the added benefit of long-term financial and political returns. If the UK further education sector is added to this equation, then the economic impact of post-secondary education is of truly startling proportions.

Whatever perspective you take, it is obvious that educational institutions require managing and, consequently, this series has been produced to facilitate that end. The editors have striven to identify authors who are distinguished practitioners in their own right and can also write. The authors have been given the challenge of producing essentially practical handbooks which combine appropriate theory and contextual material with many examples of good practice and guidance.

The topics chosen are of key importance to educational management and stand at the forefront of current debate. Some of these topics have never been covered in depth before and all of them are equally applicable to further as well as higher education. The editors are firmly of the belief that the UK distinction between these sectors will continue to blur and will be replaced, as in many other countries, by a continuum where the management issues are entirely common.

Since the mid-1980s, both of the editors have been involved with a management development programme for senior staff from HEIs throughout the world. Every year the participants quickly learn that we share the same problems and that similar solutions are normally applicable. Political and cultural differences may on occasion be important, but are often no more than an overlying veneer. Hence, this series will be of considerable relevance and value to post-secondary educational managers in many countries.

The members of post-secondary educational institutions are almost entirely dependent upon information – information which flows within the institution, between institutions and increasingly on a global scale. We are all affected. No one can escape this information tidal wave and probably no one would want to do so. The primary brief for this volume, therefore, was to produce a book on the management of information for non-information specialists, a book which we could all turn to whatever our jobs or disciplines, a book in which we could all find something of value and assistance. The editors have achieved this task superbly.

Judith Elkin and Derek Law have assembled a team of experts who have worked systematically from the broad horizons of the international context, via the UK national scene to the situation in educational institutions. Having reached this level, they deal with a variety of key topics of immense practical importance such as developing an information strategy, managing information in research, applying technology to learning and the knotty problem of intellectual property rights. Then the volume concludes with a look into the future – a future which will almost certainly be with us far more quickly than we currently think.

David Warner
David Palfreyman

LIST OF FIGURES

PREFACE

Information is the key to the modern age. The new age of
information offers possibilities for the future limited only by the
boundaries of our imaginations. The potential of the new electronic
networks is breathtaking – the prospect of change as widespread
and fundamental as the agricultural and industrial revolutions of
earlier eras.

> (UK Prime Minister, Tony Blair in *Our Information Age*)

Information underpins all the activities of further and higher education: teaching, research, administration, business development and
strategic planning. Colleges and universities need more than ever
before to ensure that information is managed effectively and efficiently. Since the new Labour government came into power in the UK
in May 1997, considerable attention has been paid to the concept
of the information society and education and lifelong learning.
Two key documents underpin government policies: *Our Information
Age: The Government's Vision* and *The Learning Age: A Renaissance for
a New Britain*. They set out the government's intention to enable
people to take advantage of the new information age concentrating
on five key areas: transforming education, widening access, promoting competition and competitiveness, fostering equality and modernizing government. Their vision is explored more fully in Chapter 2.

The emerging information and communication technologies frame
the new literacy, and the successful communities of tomorrow will be
those who, given access, are informed and educated in the use of
these technologies. There will be a need to help people at risk because
they lack the skills and to provide them with the tools to deal with
information. Information literacy will be at the heart of the educational system as a whole and be seen as an investment in people.

Further and higher education will play an increasingly strong and
fundamental role in the economic and cultural life of the regions
and the nation and the way that both sectors are managed and how
they collaborate within the wider community will be central to the

well-being of all. The effective and efficient management of information will be crucial for these institutions to survive and grow. This book looks at the management of information in administration, research, teaching and learning and discusses issues surrounding information strategies, intellectual property and the concept of hybrid and electronic libraries to underpin teaching, learning and research. The messages in all chapters are equally applicable across the whole of the further and higher education sector.

The book begins with Nick Moore's comparative study of national information policies from an international perspective, contrasting the various stages of development of such policies within the European Union (EU) and looking at developments in other parts of the world, particularly demonstrating the lead taken by Singapore. In Chapter 2 Judith Elkin sets the national scene in the UK, exploring some of the current government reports and initiatives quoted at the beginning of this preface and exploring the role of information and communication technologies (ICTs) in our future society. In Chapter 3 she highlights the need for all organizations and institutions to manage information efficiently and effectively, looking at knowledge management concepts and analysing recent further and higher education reports and initiatives which underpin teaching, learning and research. In Chapter 4 Ann Hughes explores the need for information strategies from her position as Information Strategies Coordinator for the Joint Information Systems Committee (JISC). She gives a brief history of information strategies and a summary of the first phase of the JISC Information Strategies Initiative, including the pilot sites and what was learnt from them. The extension of the project to nine 'exemplar sites' and the possible future developments are outlined.

In Chapter 5 John O'Donovan highlights the importance of collecting, organizing, analysing and disseminating information as essential for good management and decision making and provides a framework of ideas, concepts, views, practical tips and advice that can be brought to bear on the day-to-day activities of administrators. In Chapter 6 David Squires concentrates on information in research, looking at the rationale for using ICT* in research, in terms of information access, new publication mechanisms, an improved democratic research culture and efficiency and effectiveness. He bases his comments on a research study carried out at King's College

---

* ICT (Information and Communication Technologies) and CIT or C&IT (Communications and Information Technology) are interchangeable terms used by different educational sectors and government departments. No attempt has been made to harmonize them and the contributors have used the acronym with which they are familiar.

London. In Chapter 7 Alan Staley looks at information in support of learning, using Kolb's Learning Cycle as a framework. He makes links between academia and the workplace and between theory and practice in the use of appropriate technology in supporting the student. In Chapter 8 Derek Law challenges universities and colleges to take intellectual property rights more seriously and to consider the implications of this 'complex and dangerous' area of activity, particularly when compounded within an electronic environment. In Chapter 9 William Foster surveys issues surrounding the development of the electronic and hybrid library and assesses the impact that changes from a print to a networked electronic environment will have on teaching, learning and research and the implications for the future role of librarians.

It is perhaps important to stress that the book offers no 'right' answers. Some chapters give overviews, others explain particular research or policy, some offer advice and guidance. All are intended to provoke thought as to how universities and colleges operate. Collectively they stress the need for information strategies. Just as important is the need to integrate such strategies with other institutional strategies. All too often this is not done, sometimes with faintly comical results. For example, in the UK it is increasingly common to have an information technology (IT) strategy which involves wiring up halls of residence to give students access to the campus network. At the same time it is equally common to have a student pastoral policy which guarantees a place in halls of residence to first year students. Taken together – or more accurately because they are not taken together – the consequence is that those least able to use the network are given access to it and as soon as they have the skills to use it, the access is removed as they move out into houses and flats. In the same way the Estates Strategy rarely considers the implications of new teaching technologies for the future of large lecture spaces.

Inevitably a work such as this also excludes some areas. The very pervasiveness of information makes it almost impossible to draw sensible boundaries around the subject. No mention is made of the recreational use of information and whether this is a legitimate use of institutional resource. More could be made of the need for continuous staff training and development at all levels as technology spreads. Nothing is said of the growing market for smart cards and of the information component which they may include.

Further and higher education exist in a rapidly changing environment. It is impossible to reflect an up to the moment view of some changes. For up to date information on projects the authors recommend visiting the Web sites cited.

In short, this book is meant to open up the topic of information management and to encourage reflection on one's own institution and how it is dealing with the lifeblood of its activity.

Judith Elkin
Derek Law

NOTES ON CONTRIBUTORS

Judith Elkin is the Dean of the Faculty of Computing, Information and English, University of Central England in Birmingham. Her particular interest is in raising the profile of information professionals, by attracting high-quality students to undergraduate and Masters courses, offering better opportunities for continuing professional development and creating a sound research base. At UCE, she heads a team of academics and researchers concerned with communication in the widest sense, highlighting the importance of access to information and information handling in the world today. Judith is a member of the Library and Information Commission and its Research Committee. She was a member of the Higher Education Funding Councils' (HEFC) Research Assessment panel for Library and Information Management in 1992 and 1996 and will chair the 2001 panel.

William Foster is a head of teaching, learning and quality for the School of Information Studies at the University of Central England in Birmingham and Course Director of the MA/MSc Information and Library Studies (part-time). He was Academic Adviser to TAP in 1995–8, one of the eLib projects on training and awareness in networks, and has just finished coediting a book on academic culture change in networked libraries. He has worked in academic, public and special libraries and has previous experience of implementing library management systems and Online Public Access Catalogue (OPAC) design. He currently teaches in the areas of information retrieval, technical services and electronic library developments.

Ann Hughes is the JISC Information Strategies Coordinator and produced the *Guidelines for Developing an Information Strategy – The*

Sequel. Based at the University of Nottingham, she works with a wide range of higher education institutions to develop their information strategies. As part of the JISC Information Strategies Initiative she runs workshops and conferences, contributes to journals and has presented papers at conferences both in the UK and abroad. A graduate of the Open University, her career has developed through a variety of senior administrative and managerial posts in both higher and further education.

Derek Law is Director of Information Strategy at the University of Strathclyde. For most of the 1990s he was a member of the JISC and its predecessors, where he became closely associated with the development of nationally networked information and the various issues surrounding that subject. He was a founder member of the Association for Learning and Teaching and chaired the 1992 and 1996 Research Assessment Exercise panels in Library and Information Management. A visiting professor both at Sheffield University and the University of Central England in Birmingham, he is a regular author and lecturer on topics related to information management and the information society. He is at present a member of the Library and Information Commission and is treasurer of the International Federation of Library Associations.

Nick Moore is Professor of Information Policy at City University in London. He spent eight years with the Policy Studies Institute developing a programme of research into the policy issues raised by the development of information societies. He also spent two years with the British Council studying the development of information societies in East Asia. He is the managing partner in Acumen, a research consultancy specializing in information policy issues.

John O'Donovan began his career in university administration in 1981, after postgraduate and postdoctoral research at the University of Newcastle upon Tyne. For most of his career he has been involved in providing administrative support to the planning, policy and resourcing functions. He has always had a great interest in management information and its role in supporting the decision-making processes in universities. John is currently Academic Secretary at the University of Sheffield, which means that he is responsible for the leadership of a large administrative department in one of the UK's top research-led universities.

David Squires is a reader in Educational Computing, School of Education, King's College London. He has been involved since 1979 in the design and evaluation of software for use in educational settings. His current research is focused on theories of learning and the design and evaluation of educational software, the teacher as a virtual presence in networked environments, and the use of ICT in academic research. Research in the latter area has been supported by King's College (1992–3) and the British Library Research and Innovation Centre (1993–6).

Alan Staley is Head of Research in the Learning Methods Unit at the University of Central England in Birmingham. His major research interest is the appropriate use of learning technology within higher education to improve the quality of student learning. He is currently the project manager of a four-year Computer Supported Experiential Learning project which aims to identify best practice for the use of a number of technologies alongside traditional classroom-based teaching methods.

1

THE INTERNATIONAL FRAMEWORK OF INFORMATION POLICIES

Nick Moore

In years to come, we will look back on the 1990s as the time when we learned how to use information to transform the shape of our lives. The impetus for this has undoubtedly been the development of information and communication technology as a powerful and flexible resource that can be used to improve nearly all aspects of life. At the end of the twentieth century we have had forty years in which to consolidate our ability to use a technology that continues to fall in price as quickly as it expands in capacity. Countries all over the world are now trying to transform themselves into information societies – societies that can grow and prosper through the more effective use of information and its associated technologies.

The global policy response

One of the interesting things about the changes that are taking place is the fact that formal frameworks of policy are being established to steer the development of information societies. There can be few other examples of technological change stimulating formal policy creation in order to bring about social change.

The movement began in the USA during the 1992 presidential election campaign when Vice-President-Elect Al Gore set out his ideas for developing information superhighways. By this he meant a network of telecommunications that would enable the USA to communicate and use flows of information in a wide variety of ways. The use of the term 'superhighways' was no accident – Al Gore's father was a politician who is credited with launching the development of the network of interstate highways in the USA. The idea became accepted as the National Information Infrastructure and formed a major part of the programme of the first Clinton administration.[1]

In Europe, Jacques Delors recognized the potential threat of such a development to the competitiveness of the European economy and, in his final White Paper as President of the Commission,[2] he set out his ideas for developing a comparable European network of high-capacity telecommunications. Since then there have been numerous follow-up reports, studies, policies and action programmes designed to increase Europe's capacity to exploit information as an economic and, increasingly, a social resource.[3]

At that time, in the early 1990s, Singapore was the only other country to have well-developed plans for a fully fledged information society.[4] These originated in a longer term process of economic restructuring and owed little to the ideas of Al Gore or Jacques Delors. Indeed, Gore and Delors could have learned a great deal from the approach that was being followed by Singapore.

Since then, many countries have grasped the need to make a rapid transition to become information-intensive societies and there has been a steady flow of information policies and vision statements defining the goals of information societies and setting out programmes that will enable countries to attain the goals.

Common goals

One of the most interesting things is the similarity in the goals of information policy. Countries large and small, developed and undeveloped, capitalist and socialist, all share a set of aspirations that are remarkably similar.[5] The first priority is an efficient, high-capacity telecommunications system that is universally accessible. Without this, the scope for developing an information society is very limited. These telecommunications systems are often referred to as the backbone of an information society. It would be more accurate to describe them as the nervous system through which messages can be transmitted and on which the whole body, or society, depends. The second goal is the development of an economy in which organizations in both the private and public sector use information as a resource to raise levels of productivity and to improve competitiveness. At one level, the intention is to improve the efficiency of existing organizations. At a more fundamental level, however, the aim is to restructure the economy, moving into higher value-added industries that, almost by definition, are more information intensive in their operation.

Closely related to this is the need to develop the quality of the education and training system to satisfy the demand for skilled labour. Increasingly, however, it is recognized that to create a society in which information is used for the common good, it is necessary to develop a culture in which there is a genuine, and continuing, desire to learn. There are political goals, with information societies seen as a way of strengthening democracy through the development of an informed citizenry. And finally there is a cultural dimension with countries trying to use the information society to strengthen local culture and to protect it from the incursion of a bland, global culture.

Different motivations

In developed countries the main motivation comes from fear.[6] Countries are afraid that they will lose their dominant position in a rapidly changing global economy, and the information society is seen as a way of avoiding this. Associated with this there is a concern about social disruption brought about by high levels of unemployment and by other structural changes in society. This produces pressure to exploit an economic opportunity in the hope that, by maintaining or, if possible, increasing levels of national income it will be possible to prevent social dislocation and, critically, bring more of the workforce into employment.

Outside the developed countries the motivation is different. Here the move towards an information society is seen as the next step in a process of economic development within a competitive global economic system. Motivation comes from a realization of what might be achieved rather than from a fear of what might be lost.

Different mechanisms

There are also marked differences in the ways in which countries have gone about repositioning themselves as information societies. At one extreme is the neo-liberal or market-driven approach. Here, market forces are all important and the state plays a minor role, simply ensuring that the conditions are right for the private sector and stepping in wherever there is market failure. Clearly in such circumstances, profit is the most important determinant of the direction that the information society takes.

At the other extreme there are the dirigiste or interventionist approaches of countries like Korea and Singapore. Here the state is seen as the key player, working in partnership with the private sector to achieve a set of goals that have been established by the state. The public sector is an active partner, undertaking investment and managing both risk and competition so that private and public goals can be achieved successfully.[7]

Developments in Europe

Europe has been in the forefront of developments towards an information society. Progress has been helped greatly by a favourable set of conditions that, together, have provided a firm foundation on which development could take place. First, and perhaps most important, nearly all of Europe is served by efficient telecommunications systems. Further, the introduction of competition, following the European Commission's Directive in 1990,[8] along with technological advances, has meant that the overall levels of productivity in the telecommunications systems have risen significantly. As a result, costs have reduced, capacity has expanded and it has been possible to finance the necessary capital investment largely out of revenue income.

Businesses and households have also been quite willing to invest in computers and other hardware. As a result most European companies have access to computers and make significant use of information and communications technology.[9] Also, the number of European households that own a personal computer (PC) is growing at over 30 per cent each year.[10,11] The overall number of PCs in Europe was forecast to double between 1997 and 2000.[12] Europe also has a strong information industry. It is true that the European hardware industry has been unable to compete with companies in North America and East Asia, but there are significant strengths in the software industry and, particularly, in the information content industries of publishing and broadcasting. Here, European companies compete very successfully in global markets. All these factors are reinforced by a highly educated population supported by strong education and training services, and by well-established democratic structures that support open, information-intensive societies.

Together, these factors have given European countries the potential to create the economic, social, political and cultural structures that together constitute an information society.

The role of the European Commission

The European Commission has played an important part in stimulating information society developments within the member states. The Commission gave such developments a high priority in the mid-1990s at a time when others were only beginning to become aware of the need for change. It created a framework of policy within which development could be planned and it stimulated the process through an extensive range of support actions. Between 1995 and 1998 there was, however, a significant shift in the priorities of the Commission. At first, development was seen in almost exclusively economic terms. The goal was to ensure that European companies were able to compete successfully in a global economy. To do this they would have to be able to raise productivity levels through the better use of information and communication technology.[13,14]

As the decade progressed, however, the emphasis broadened and the goal is now to promote a much wider process of social and cultural change. Here, the vision has been established by the High Level Expert Group established by Commissioner Padraig Flynn,[15,16] supported by the Information Society Forum.[17,18] Their vision of the European information society is much more wide ranging and is concerned with creating a learning society in which the benefits of information and communications technology will be used, and controlled, by everyone.

The economic dimension cannot, however, be forgotten, rather the focus of policy has broadened to encompass social, political and cultural issues. On this basis, it now becomes clear that the development of a European information society involves policy at three levels. At the industrial level we need to create effective information industries that can compete in an increasingly important global market while also satisfying the information demands that arise within Europe. At the organizational level we must create a culture in which organizations in the public and private sector use information as a resource to improve productivity, to increase effectiveness and to raise levels of competitiveness. Finally, at the social level we must develop an information-intensive social system that enables people to use information constructively in their roles as citizens, consumers and participants in the democratic process.

Running parallel to these three levels is a need to evolve a framework of legislation and regulation that will enable the society to function equitably and consistently within a global context.

The responses of the member states

The member states have responded in different ways. In part the differences reflect the variations in economic capacity of the different countries. They also reflect differences in political philosophy and views of the role of the state in shaping economic and social change. It is possible to identify three groups: the Northerners, who have adopted a formal, policy-driven approach in which the state has taken the lead; the Southerners, in which the state and the private sector share responsibility within a relatively unstructured system; and a Middle Europe group, in which a belief in the power of markets is being replaced by a more interventionist model.

The Northern group is making the most rapid progress towards an information society. Denmark, Finland, the Netherlands and Sweden are ahead of the other member states in almost all respects. Each country has carefully worked-out policies that are based on thorough analysis of the issues. In each case this analysis was undertaken by a high-level group consisting of people from within government and experts from industry and the academic world. These groups analysed the problem, defined a vision of what an information society should be and set out a programme of action to be pursued by the government, working in close collaboration with the private sector.[19-24] In each of the countries the development of these policies was given political backing at the highest level. In Sweden, for example, the prime minister chaired the commission of inquiry for the first year and gave the policy his personal backing. In other countries, the implementation of the policies was steered by senior ministers, again working with clear support from the prime minister.

These countries also benefited from an early start. In Finland, consideration of the issues began in earnest following an Organization for Economic Cooperation and Development (OECD) report in 1992. In the other countries, serious policy development began in 1993–4 with key reports published in 1994 and programmes of action beginning soon after. Another common characteristic is the broad view of developments that was adopted from the outset. Each country was concerned with much more than economic development. Social transformation was the clear imperative and, perhaps because of this, the state was seen to play a key role in the process of development. Key to the success of the policies was coordination and joint development. There was a recognition that the creation of an information society involved several government departments and, while one might be given the responsibility to lead the process, high-level coordination was essential. This broad view also meant that a wide range of initiatives was set in train to bring about the changes. Steps were taken to secure the commitment of the private sector, particularly in the creation of the information infrastructure, but the programme of activities extended well beyond to involve the whole of the public sector, particularly local municipalities. There was a strong sense of the government committing resources in order to lever investment from the private sector and this strategy appears to have been successful.

In Denmark, for example, the Ministry of Research is leading a government initiative to develop, by 2000, self-service entry-points to all parts of the government service and, to facilitate this, they made all forms for citizens and businesses available on the Internet by the end of 1998. Denmark is also committed to the creation, by 2001, of a cohesive digital research library structure that will harness the capacity of the main libraries in the country.

In Finland, the National Post gave everyone an email address to stimulate the take-up of electronic mail. Finland also developed the concept of a computer driving licence – a basic test of the essential skills required to use personal computers. About 25,000 people passed the test in the three years following its introduction in 1995 and it has since been developed as a European licence.

In the Netherlands the government supported the creation of SeniorWeb, an organization designed to promote the use of information and communication technologies among older people. It offers training, support and a starter pack which consists of a computer, modem and Internet connection. The government also has an ambitious programme to integrate information and communication technology into all levels of the Dutch education system.

In Sweden, Toppledarforum has been established to promote electronic communication between administrations, citizens and local businesses. Sweden has also instituted a major training and reskilling programme to meet shortages of skilled labour in the information technology industries and to re-equip unemployed people with the abilities they need to move into jobs in an expanding sector of the economy.

Denmark, Finland and Sweden, along with Norway, which is similar in many respects,[25] have gone a long way towards redefining themselves as Nordic information societies. They have developed globally successful industries that excel in high value-added, information-intensive production; they have begun the process of social, cultural and political transformation and they have built on a tradition of high-quality education. In the first decade of the twenty-first century these Nordic countries will be the first to make the full transformation to information societies. The Netherlands shares many of the characteristics of these Nordic countries and fully justifies its place among the Northern group.

The Southern group consists of Greece, Italy and Spain. Portugal shares some of the characteristics of the Southern group but in other respects it is rather different. Within the Southern group there appears to be a reluctance to give a high priority to information society developments and, while there is some activity within national governments and local and regional administrations, there is nothing like the impetus that is a characteristic of the Northern group.

That being said, there are two exceptions which, together, suggest that even in this group there are signs of change. Most significant is Portugal which has produced a very thorough, wide-ranging policy document that provides a very positive framework for the development of an information society.[26] The second example is Italy, which is also changing. The government has established an Information Society Forum that has published an overall plan;[27] this has been followed up by a statement on infrastructures from the Ministry of Industry and Communication.[28]

In Greece, however, there has been no noticeable attempt to develop an information policy. It is possible that the need to manage a major upgrade and extension of the telecommunications infrastructure has preoccupied the policy makers but this does not fully explain the lack of policy impetus. It is perhaps more likely that the lack of policy is a consequence of a political and administrative tradition that is very different from that found in Northern Europe. If that is so, it serves to make Portugal's Green Paper and Italy's Information Society Forum all the more significant.

The lack of a formal policy, however, has not held up the development of some impressive applications in these countries. In Spain, for example, the government has developed a very successful system for the payment of unemployment benefits through automated teller machines, using smart cards and fingerprint identification. In Italy the Ministry of Finance has introduced an electronic income tax form – something that other countries have wanted to do but have hesitated because of the complexity.

In Portugal there is an extensive public information programme delivered through kiosks. Originally intended just for one-way communication it is now being made interactive. The government has also designated seven digital cities that will serve as laboratories to explore the application of information and communication technology.

Despite the progress made with these individual applications, there is a general lack of coordination in these Southern European countries and this will be a barrier to effective future development. Much of the value of technological applications in the information society lies in the opportunities they offer to cut across departmental boundaries and to take a holistic view of an individual's needs. Without coordination and a joint approach to solutions, much of this potential value will be lost.

The Middle Europeans consist of a large group of countries: Austria, Belgium, France, Germany, Ireland, Luxembourg and the United Kingdom. It is possible that Portugal should be included in this group. These are the late starters which have only recently begun to give high priority to the development of a coordinated set of information society policies. Germany and Luxembourg published their information society policies in 1996.[29,30] Austria, Belgium, France, Ireland and Portugal published documents in 1997;[31-5] the United Kingdom produced its first consolidated policy statement in 1998.[36] It is interesting to speculate on the reasons for the delay. In some cases, notably Austria, priority in the early part of the 1990s was being given to the infrastructure and the need to develop an effective telecommunications service. In Ireland and Portugal a process of rapid and seemingly sustainable economic growth has focused political attention on information-based economic development and from this has come a wider concern about the societal implications. It is possible that in Belgium and Germany the split between the federal level of government and the states discouraged the creation of a national policy. Certainly in both countries there are well-developed policies at the level of the state administrations.

In France and the United Kingdom, a change of government has brought a change in thinking about the need to define policy on issues such as the development of an information society and this has been accompanied by a change in thinking about the respective roles of the state and the private sector. Broadly, a belief in the power and importance of market forces has been replaced by a more interventionist form of thinking. It is possible that the change of administration in Germany will produce a similar change there. Whatever the reasons, these countries are following three or four years behind their Nordic neighbours in the development of information society policies.

Close examination of some of the policies also reveals a degree of superficiality when compared to those of countries like Sweden or the Netherlands. A possible exception is Portugal, where the policy was developed through an extensive process of public consultation, and Ireland, where the policy document was produced by a specially formed Commission. In contrast the policies of France and the United Kingdom could be criticized for being political statements that lack any real grounding in analysis and careful reflection by knowledge-able partners. Despite this apparent superficiality, the policies have been given a high level of political backing. In many cases the policies have been produced and published by the prime minister's office and the prime minister has been closely involved in the pro-motion of the policy documents and in some of the higher profile activities that are associated with them. In the case of the United Kingdom, the policy statement is less a vision of the future, although this is its subtitle. Rather, it draws together a number of develop-ments that have been put in place during the previous four or five years. It is, therefore, a rationalization of what has been taking place and, as such, provides a basis for further development.

Compared with the Northern group of countries, the Middle Euro-peans demonstrate a marked lack of coordination in the development of the policies. Whereas the leading group adopted a coordinated approach within government from the outset, a common feature of the Middle group is the development of separate policies by each individual ministry. In France, for example, each department has been asked to develop its own policies following the publication of the national plan. This seems to run counter to the idea of a coordin-ated, coherent approach to a set of developments that cut across established departmental boundaries.

Despite this lack of a coordinated policy framework, each country has developed a range of applications to promote the development of an information society. In Austria, all schools have been given 20 hours of free Internet connection a week and the Ministry of Eco-nomic Affairs makes available grants to enable small firms to buy in consultancy to develop telematic applications. In Belgium much of the development is taking place at a local level: in Brussels there is a network linking the most important social, scientific and economic institutions, while in the Charleroi Region a research and training institute has been established to diffuse expertise among companies. Local initiatives are also characteristic of developments in France. On the Plateau de Vercours it is possible to buy stored value cards that provide Internet access in post offices. At a national level, Agence France Presse has created Mercure, an electronic news service to deliver information to local authorities over the Internet. In Ger-many the Ministry of Education, Science, Research and Technology has established a competition to stimulate the use of multimedia among older people, while in Bavaria, a high-capacity network has been established linking medical centres to enable clinicians to communicate while also providing an electronic information source for patients. Telecom Éireann in Ireland has awarded a major grant to the town of Ennis to support its development as an information-age town. Each household will have a free telephone connection, voicemail, reduced cost computers, modems and smart electronic cash transfer, all designed to test the universal development of information-society applications. In the United Kingdom the government has announced two networks, one linking schools, the other linking public libraries. Together they will complement JANET, the Joint Academic Network connecting higher education institutions, and are designed to promote the concept of lifelong learning.

Developments outside Europe

There are numerous other examples of information society developments. In the USA there are two parallel strands for the development of policy: one within government, the other acting in an advisory role outside the formal structure. The Information Infrastructure Task Force was established by the president to articulate and implement the administration's vision for the National Information Infrastructure. It consists of high-level representatives of the federal agencies that play a major role in the development and application of information and telecommunications technologies. As such, it is part of the executive arm of government. It operates under the White House Office of Science and Technology Policy and the National Economic Council. The Advisory Council on the National Information Infrastructure is a larger body that provides advice on technical and other matters. Strictly it advises the Secretary of Commerce on matters concerning the development of the national information infrastructure. The 37 members represented a wide range of interest groups and stakeholders. The Council delivered its final report in February 1996.[37] The work of these two bodies has provided a framework for the development of a wide range of applications.

The task of developing a vision of Canada as an information society was delegated to the Information Highway Advisory Council drawn from a range of constituencies. This body produced one of the most thorough and authoritative documents about information societies.[38]

In Australia the task of developing the plans for an Australian information society was originally given to a group that was similar in composition to the Canadian Advisory Council. Before it had done much work, however, there was a change of government and the group was suspended. It was replaced by the Information Policy

Advisory Council which, in August 1997, produced a report setting out the vision for a 'new commonwealth of information'.[39] This identified a number of Australia's comparative strengths and encouraged the government to establish a Ministerial Council for the Information Economy, supported by the Australian National Office for the Information Economy. In 1998 the Council produced its report which takes the vision somewhat further and sets out a strategy for attaining it.[40] In the meantime, the individual states are competing with each other for the development of an infrastructure and economic framework that will attract and sustain information-intensive companies.

In Japan there is a characteristic overlapping division of responsibilities between ministries. There are two leading organizations: the Ministry of Posts and Telecommunications and the Ministry of International Trade and Industry. In addition, the Ministry for Education, Science and Culture is responsible for a number of programmes that have a bearing on the development of information policy. The Ministry of Posts and Telecommunications produced two important documents in 1994. First was a report of an inquiry conducted by the Telecommunications Council.[41] This analysed the current state of Japan's telecommunications and information infrastructure, reviewed the implications of an 'info-communications infrastructure' on society and the economy and suggested an approach towards the development of the networks and the applications that would use them. This was followed by a White Paper,[42] which advocated the development of an 'info-communications economy and society' built around sophisticated telecommunications and with a heavy reliance on multimedia. Meanwhile at the Ministry of International Trade and Industry, the Information Industry Committee of the Industrial Structure Council issued a report that argued that Japan should take further steps to exploit information and communications technology throughout society. In May 1994 the Ministry of International Trade and Industry published its response to this report.[43] This assessed the need to spread information technology and networks into industry, the home and into the public sector. It went on to recommend action to stimulate the use of information technology in education, research, medical and welfare service, administrative services and libraries. It also considered the need for standardization, security and the protection of intellectual property rights, concluding with recommendations for stimulating the development of multimedia software, general software and databases.

The Ministry for Education, Science and Culture has put in place a large-scale programme to raise levels of computer literacy throughout the school system. Despite its high-technology culture, computer use is not widespread in Japan. This is, no doubt, due to the difficulties in handling the three types of Japanese characters in word processing and other applications. There is now, however, a recognition of the need to catch up. The ministry has set out teaching guidelines for information literacy in elementary, middle and high schools. The ministry is also responsible for promoting database development and use and for developing scientific and technological information systems, including the National Centre for Science Information Systems which links all universities and which provides a wide range of on-line services.

While impressive, these large countries face major problems of coordination and scale. Perhaps not surprisingly, therefore, it is to a small country that we have to turn to find the most comprehensive approach to the development of an information society. In Singapore, responsibility has been placed firmly with the National Computer Board as the lead agency within government for the advancement of Singapore as an information society. The National Computer Board is a statutory board established initially with the aim of computerizing government and later charged with supervising the overall development of Singapore as an 'Intelligent Island'. It is, therefore, executive rather than advisory.

It is possible to identify four phases of development in Singapore. First, there was the *National Computerization Plan*.[44] This aimed to computerize ministries and departments to improve efficiency, effectiveness and service to the public; to expand the supply of computer professionals; and to support expansion of software and services industries. It was followed by the *National Information Technology Plan*.[45] This set out a strategic framework to develop the information technology capacity of Singapore, to build the networks and to develop applications. The third phase was *Information Technology 2000: The Intelligent Island*.[46] This was a comprehensive development plan formulated by the National Computer Board in consultation with 200 senior executives from 11 major economic sectors. It has five strategic thrusts: to develop Singapore as a global hub; to boost the national economic engine; to link communities locally and globally; to improve the quality of life in Singapore; and to enhance the potential of individuals. Finally, there is the *IT 2000 Action Plan: From Vision to Reality*.[47] This focuses on three areas of development: a wide range of applications aimed at economic sectors such as TradeNet for the import–export sector or LawNet for the legal community and includes the Library 2000 blueprint for a borderless library; middleware, reuseable common services that can be used by different sectors that ensure data security, billing, directory services, and so on; telecommunications network services with high bandwidth and universal access. In addition, there is a range of supporting actions to create the necessary social, economic, legal and regulatory environment.

These four phases have culminated in the latest encapsulation of Singapore as an information society: *Singapore ONE*.[48] This represents the next stage in the development of the Intelligent Island. *Singapore ONE* is a development plan that has two main strands: the infrastructure and the applications. The infrastructure will consist of a broadband core that will connect several local access networks. The core will be built and owned by an industrial consortium. The local access networks will be owned by Singapore Telecom and Singapore Cable Vision. The long-term aim is to provide broadband connections to the home. The applications and services are regarded as the key to the success of the venture. Developments are taking place in four areas:

* *Government*: to bring government services closer to the public through kiosks and one-stop shops.
* *Home*: mainly focused on entertainment – video on demand – personal transactions – home banking, electronic shopping – and access to electronic information services through the Internet.
* *Education*: access to multimedia teaching and learning materials for distance learning and student collaboration.
* *Business*: this includes business services – video conferencing – electronic business information, electronic commerce and teleworking.

The pilot network to support these developments was operational by 1998, mainly carrying government-originated information. During the period 1999–2004 attention will be concentrated on extension of network access and expansion of content. The National Computer Board is an executive agency. Its plans and the overall vision are developed by the board working in consultation with a wide range of individuals mainly in the industrial sector. It has been given the clear lead responsibility within the Singaporean administration. The result is an impressive example of what can be achieved and a vivid illustration of what life in an information society will be like.

Elsewhere in East Asia there has been a wave of policy formulation designed to position countries so that they can take full advantage of the twin strands of technological convergence and globalization. In almost every case, the plans received a setback with the recession of the late 1990s, but it was a pause on a longer process of transition rather than a significant turn around.

In Malaysia Dr Mahathir set out a grand vision for the creation of a 'multimedia super corridor'. This was closely identified with the prime minister's vision of Malaysia as a country that would be fully developed, economically and socially, by 2020. The multimedia super corridor was a physical space linking the capital with the new administrative centre of Putra Jaya and incorporating the new airport. It was to be fully wired with high-capacity networks and a wide range of incentives were offered to encourage high technology companies to relocate. The economic downturn has put the plans on hold at the time of writing but there are signs that the initiative is soon to be revived.

Korea, in contrast, has avoided undue reliance on one big project. Rather, the government has developed a far-reaching set of policies that together are shaping Korea as an Asian information society. The government set the overall approach in 1997 with a 'master plan for informatization'. Since then each ministry has developed its own plans within this overall framework. There has been a long series of plans, reports, white papers and vision statements to provide guidance and strategic direction. The most recent is *Korea's Vision for the Information Society*, published in 1999 and providing a summation of progress and the plans for the future.

Other countries that are developing policy frameworks for their information societies and economies include China, the Philippines, Thailand and Vietnam. Throughout the region there is a recognition of the strategic necessity of bringing about structural economic and social change to enable the countries to capitalize on the opportunities that are becoming available.

Future progress

The pace of development is accelerating and the prospect of having fully functioning information societies throughout the developed world is coming closer. Many of the newly industrialized countries are working to develop information-intensive economies that will give them a competitive advantage in a global economy.

We have largely overcome the major technological problems. This is not to say that further development is unnecessary or that it will not take place. Far from it. Simply that the technology that we now have available will permit us to do everything that we need to do in order to create an effective information society. There are continuing problems of investment and it will be a long time before we have ensured that there is universal access to information throughout Europe. But technology is no longer a barrier.

In Europe and North America the information industry is also set to continue its rapid path of expansion. The US information industry is still the global leader but since the 1980s the European information industry has grown faster than the rest of the European economy;[49] we can look forward to a time which is not far off when the information industry is a major contributor to the overall European economy. It is also very well placed to compete in the global economy. Organizations within the developed countries are using information more and more creatively as a business resource and they are becoming more effective as a result. European and American companies are leading the way in the development of knowledge management techniques.

Electronic commerce is likely to be a big driver of economic growth in the future and there are already signs that companies in North America and, to a less extent, Europe are beginning to realize the potential that is on offer.[50] In both regions governments are actively supporting the growth of electronic commerce and small countries are beginning to jump on the bandwagon: Bermuda recently announced its intention to become a centre for offshore electronic commerce.

We are also developing information-intensive social systems. Information and communications technology is being used to deliver public services more effectively and consumers now have more information available to them than ever before. We still have some way to go before we have social systems in which all citizens have easy access to authoritative information and the ability to use it. But a good start has been made. It has become clear that to function effectively, information societies need a sound legal and regulatory framework and a well-established tradition of respect for the law. The framework needs to be updated constantly to take account of changes in technology and its application and to ensure that the laws are in harmony with global laws and regulations. But the mechanisms exist to ensure that this happens. We are also beginning to extend the framework of individual rights to accommodate the intellectual rights that will define citizenship in an information society.[51]

We still have a very long way to go before we have created the kind of learning society that is envisaged in the report of the European Commission's High Level Expert Group.[52] And it will be necessary to invest much more in the whole education system so that we develop the intellectual capital that will be so important in the future global information society. We will also need to link to this a change in our culture so that we reinforce in everyone the desire to learn.

We must also recognize that the technology of global communication brings with it a considerable threat to national and local cultures. There is a real danger that the distinctive cultures, in all their richness and diversity, will become smothered by a bland global culture, manufactured in Hollywood and designed to meet the desires of the majority – desires that can be manipulated to suit the requirements of the owners of the cultural industries.

There is also a residual danger that the introduction of an information society will reinforce and deepen social exclusion rather than help to overcome it. A recent report from the US Department of Commerce[53] suggests that the gap is widening and is doing so on racial and economic lines. In Europe we already have a society in which a significant minority are excluded from the mainstream of social benefit through poor education, lack of employment, low incomes, disability and poor housing. We must work hard to ensure that the creation of an information society does not exclude them further. Equally, we must begin to think about a global policy framework to ensure that the development of information societies does not increase the North-South divide.

Notes

1 Information Infrastructure Task Force (1993) *National Information Infrastructure: An Agenda for Action*. Washington, DC: US Government Publications Office.
2 European Commission (1993) *Growth, Competitiveness and Employment: The Challenges and Ways Forward into the 21st Century*, White Paper COM (93) 700 Final. Brussels: European Commission.
3 European Commission (1995) *The European Society in Action*. Brussels: European Commission.
4 National Computer Board (1991) *Information Technology 2000: The Intelligent Island*. Singapore: Government of Singapore.
5 N. Moore (1997) Policies for an information society, *Political Quarterly*, 68(3): 276–83.
6 Ibid.
7 Ibid.
8 European Commission (1990) *Directive on Competition in the Market for Telecommunications Services* (90.388/EEC). Brussels: European Commission.
9 Spectrum (1998) *Moving into the Information Age: International Benchmarking Study 1998*. London: Department of Trade and Industry.
10 Financial Times (1998) *The European Multimedia Business*. London: Financial Times, Telecoms and Media Publishing.
11 *European Computer Literacy: The 1997 Olivetti Personal Computer Report, 1997*.
12 Ibid.
13 European Council (1994) *Europe and the Global Information Society: Recommendations to the European Council* (Bangemann Report). Brussels: European Council.
14 European Commission (1994) *Europe's Way to the Information Society: An Action Plan*, COM (94) 347 Final. Brussels: European Commission.

15 European Commission, High Level Expert Group (1996) *Building the Information Society for Us All: Interim Report*. Brussels: European Commission.
16 European Commission, High Level Expert Group (1997) *Building the Information Society for Us All*. Brussels: European Commission.
17 European Commission, Information Society Forum (1996) *Networks for People and their Communities*. Brussels: European Commission.
18 European Commission, Information Society Forum (1997) *Report*. Brussels: European Commission.
19 Government of the Netherlands (1994) *An Action Programme for Electronic Highways*. The Hague: Government of the Netherlands.
20 Ministry of Finance (1994) *Finland towards the Information Society: A National Strategy*. Helsinki: Finnish Government.
21 Ministry of Research (1994) *Information Society 2000: Report from the Committee on the Information Society by the Year 2000*. Copenhagen: Danish Government.
22 Ministry of Research and Information Technology (1995) *From Vision to Action: Info-society 2000*. Copenhagen: Danish Government.
23 Swedish Information Technology Commission (1994) *Information Technology: Wings to Human Ability*. Stockholm: Prime Minister's Office.
24 Government of the Netherlands (1995) *Vision on Acceleration*. The Hague: Government of the Netherlands. (Note: an earlier version of this paper was presented at the Federacion Espanola de Asociaciones de Especialistas en Informacion, Bibliotec, Documentacion & Archivos (FESABID) conference, as: Los Sistemas de Informacion al Servicio de la Sociedad (1998) *Into the Information Age*. Valencia.)
25 Ministry of Government Administration (1994) *Central Government Information Policy*. Oslo: Ministry of Government Administration.
26 (1997) *Information Society: The Green Paper on the Information Society in Portugal*. Lisbon: Missao para sociedade da informacao.
27 (1997) *Promotion of Information Society Development: A Reference Scheme*. Rome: Information Society Forum, Italy.
28 (1998) *Information Society Infrastructures*. Rome: Ministry of Industry and Communication, Italy.
29 Ministry of Education, Science and Research (1996) *Info 2000: Germany's Way to the Information Society*. Bonn: Ministry of Education, Science and Research.
30 (1996) *Report on the Information Society in Luxembourg*. Grand Duchy of Luxembourg.
31 (1997) *Information Society: Report of the Working Group of the Austrian Federal Government*. Vienna: Austrian Federal Government.
32 (1997) *Federal Action Plan for the Development of an Information Society*. Brussels: Government of Belgium.
33 (1997) *Government Action Plan to Prepare the Entry of France in the Information Society*. Paris: Office of the Prime Minister.
34 Information Society Commission (1997) *National Information Society Strategy and Action Plan*. Dublin: Government of Ireland.
35 (1997) *Information Society: The Green Paper on the Information Society in Portugal*. Lisbon: Missao para sociedade da informacao.

36 Central Office of Information (1998) *Our Information Age: The Government's Vision.* London: Central Office of Information.
37 Advisory Council on the National Information Infrastructure (1996) *A Nation of Opportunity: Final Report of the United States Advisory Council on the National Information Infrastructure.* Washington, DC: Advisory Council on the National Information Infrastructure.
38 Information Highway Advisory Council (1995) *Connection, Community, Content: The Challenge of the Information Highway.* Ottawa: Ministry of Supply and Service.
39 Information Policy Advisory Council (1997) *A National Policy Framework for Structural Adjustment within the New Commonwealth of Information.* Canberra: Information Policy Advisory Council.
40 Ministerial Council for the Information Economy (1998) *Towards an Australian Strategy for the Information Economy.* Canberra: Australian National Office for the Information Economy.
41 Ministry of Posts and Telecommunications, Telecommunications Council (1994) *Reforms toward the Intellectually Creative Society of the 21st Century.* Tokyo: Ministry of Posts and Telecommunications.
42 Ministry of Posts and Telecommunications (1994) *Communications in Japan.* Tokyo: Ministry of Posts and Telecommunications.
43 Ministry of International Trade and Industry (1994) *Program for Advanced Information Infrastructure.* Tokyo: Ministry of Trade and Industry.
44 National Computer Board (1981) *National Computerization Plan.* Singapore: Government of Singapore.
45 National Computer Board (1986) *National Information Technology Plan.* Singapore: Government of Singapore.
46 National Computer Board (1991) op. cit.
47 National Computer Board (1995) *IT 2000 Action Plan: From Vision to Reality.* Singapore: Government of Singapore.
48 National Computer Board (1996) *Singapore ONE.* Singapore: Government of Singapore.
49 European Commission, Information Market Observatory (1997) *Annual Report on the European Information Market.* Luxembourg: European Commission.
50 Spectrum op. cit.
51 N. Moore (1998) Rights and responsibilities in an information society, *Journal of Information Law and Technology,* 1 http://elj.warwick.ac.uk/jilt/infosoc/98_1moor/
52 European Commission, High Level Expert Group (1997) op. cit.
53 (1999) *Falling through the Net: A report on the telecommunications and information gap in America.* US Department of Commerce.

2

INFORMATION: THE UK NATIONAL SCENE

Judith Elkin

The vision

Since the new Labour government came into power in the United Kingdom in May 1997, there has been considerable attention paid to the concept of the Information Society and education and lifelong learning. Two documents underpin current policies: *Our Information Age: The Government's Vision*[1] and *The Learning Age: A Renaissance for a New Britain.*[2] *Our Information Age*, published in 1998, was the government's response to a number of earlier consultative documents and initiatives. It was the government's policy statement on how it intends to enable people to take advantage of the new information age, concentrating on five key areas: transforming education, widening access, promoting competition and competitiveness, fostering equality and modernizing government.

> Britain's dynamism, creativity, drive and enterprise fit closely with the new age of information. English is the common language of the Internet. I am determined to ensure that Britain is at the forefront of these new developments, as companies around the world link up in new forms of electronic commerce and individuals increasingly connect electronically, cutting across the restrictions of time and distance. The wired society is no longer a futurist's dream – but the practical new reality . . . Information technology is central to our key priority of improving education for all.

Education and the information age will support and reinforce each other. The information age will transform education, at all levels and for all ages. Education in turn will equip people with the necessary skills to profit from the information age ... Information and communication technologies (ICT) are learning tools, just like the blackboard or the textbook. But they bring three major advantages that will enhance the quality of our children's education. They are personal – allowing individuals to progress at their own pace. They are global – taking learners to new sources of knowledge from across the world. And they are economical – automating routine tasks and freeing teachers to concentrate on teaching itself.[3]

Also published in 1998, *The Learning Age* spelt out the government's policies on education and training, with specific reference to the concept of lifelong learning:

Learning is the key to prosperity – for each of us as individuals, as well as for the nation as a whole. Investment in human capital will be the foundation of success in the knowledge-based economy of the twenty-first century. This is why the Government has put learning at the heart of its ambition ... Learning throughout life will build human capital by encouraging acquisition of knowledge and skills and emphasising creativity and imagination. The fostering of an enquiring mind and the love of learning are essential for our future success. To achieve stable and sustainable growth, we will need a well-educated, well-equipped and adaptable labour force. To cope with rapid change and the challenge of the information and communication age, we must ensure that people can return to learning throughout their lives. We cannot rely on a small elite, no matter how highly educated or highly paid. Instead, we need the creativity, enterprise and scholarship of all our people.[4]

We are in a new age – the age of information and of global competition ... The Industrial Revolution was built on capital investment in plant and machinery, skills and hard physical labour ... The information and knowledge-based revolution of the twenty-first century will be built on a very different foundation – investment in the intellect and creativity of people ... Our single greatest challenge is to equip ourselves for this new age with new and better skills, with knowledge and with understanding.[5]

It defined the scope of the Learning Age:

> Our vision of the Learning Age is about more than employ-
> ment. The development of a culture of learning will help to
> build a united society, assist in the creation of personal inde-
> pendence, and encourage our creativity and innovation. Learn-
> ing encompasses basic literacy to advanced scholarship. We learn
> in many different ways through formal study, reading, watch-
> ing television, going on a training course, taking an evening
> classes, at work, and from family and friends . . . The country
> has a great learning tradition. We have superb universities and
> colleges which help maintain our position as a world leader
> in technology, finance, design, manufacturing and the creative
> industries. We want more people to have the chance to experi-
> ence the richness of this tradition by participating in learning.[6]

> Our vision will be built on the following principles: investing in
> learning to benefit everyone; lifting barriers to learning; putting
> people first; sharing responsibility with employers, employees
> and the community; achieving world class standards and value
> for money; working together as the key to success.[7]

Further education is highlighted as fundamental to this government
vision:

> Further education colleges will play a key role in educating both
> young people and adults . . . Further education has demonstrated
> innovation and flexibility in response to new demands from
> individuals and businesses. Many colleges have worked imagin-
> atively to improve access, operating across a number of sites
> and working collaboratively with employers, LEAs, community
> organisations and private training providers.[8]

Higher education, too, is seen as playing a fundamental role in the
thrust towards lifelong learning and greater access:

> Higher education, offering high quality and high standards, has
> a central role to play in the Learning Age . . . Higher education
> is a major contributor to local, regional and national economic
> growth and regeneration . . . We wish universities, higher and
> further education to be beacons of learning in their communities.[9]

A number of key documents contributed to the government's vision.
Other initiatives will provide the fundamental building blocks to
delivery of that vision.

The University for Industry (Ufi)

The aim of the University for Industry (Ufi) is to complement traditional learning mechanisms by using new technology to make learning available to adults at work, at home or at local learning centres.[10] It has two strategic objectives: to stimulate demand for lifelong learning among businesses and individuals, and to promote the availability of, and improve access to, relevant, high quality and innovative learning, in particular through the use of information and communication technologies.

> Our aim is a society where people and businesses take control of their destinies to build the future . . . Everyone, regardless of their background or circumstances, should have the opportunity to take control of their own career and realise their own ambitions . . . Every business should strive to maximise its potential to compete in today's increasingly global markets . . . Learning is the key to this – the key to individual employability and business competitiveness.[11]

The Ufi is intended to help people and businesses to identify the learning they need and to access this learning in the right form, in the right place, at the right time; to give access through computers or broadcast media at home, in the workplace and through a network of learning centres in a variety of locations, in companies, colleges, schools, universities, libraries, retail outlets, training and enterprise councils. It is intended to be a part of everyday life for everyone, concentrating on basic skills, information and communication technologies, particularly for small and medium-sized businesses and specific sectors such as automotive components, multimedia, environmental technology and services and the distributive and retail trades. Part of the University for Industry's remit, as set out in *The Learning Age*, will be the concept of individualized learning accounts which 'will lead the way for people to take control of this investment in their own future'. Individual learning accounts will be built on the principles that 'individuals are best placed to choose what and how they want to learn . . . responsibility for investing in learning is shared'.[12]

The Fryer Report

The concept of lifelong learning has been promoted in some circles for a number of years. But the arguments for such a concept were brought together in the Fryer Report, *Learning for the Twenty-First Century*.[13] The National Advisory Group for Continuing Education and Lifelong Learning was established in June 1997, to advise the Secretary of State for Education and Employment on the development of a culture of lifelong learning for all, throughout the whole of the United Kingdom. The report identified the following priorities: the UK needed to develop a new learning culture, a culture of lifelong learning for all; learning must become normal and accessible, and learners must be put at the centre, taking increased ownership of their own learning and its management throughout life; a clear commitment to widening and deepening participation and achievement in learning was required, with a variety and diversity of learning opportunities and increased emphasis on the home, community and workplace as key places of learning.

A national skills agenda

The aim of the Skills Task Force is to create a national skills agenda, recognizing that:

> Productivity and social cohesion are key twin challenges facing the UK in ensuring our nation's economic success in the 21st century. At the heart of both of these challenges lies skills – for the competitiveness of our businesses and the employability of our people.[14]

To date only a preliminary report has been published, setting out the three key issues of current skills shortages, underlying skills gaps and addressing longer term needs. These are underpinned by four key themes: ensuring a strong focus on priority skills needed in national education and training provision, building on better information and a more responsive system; better targeted help for employers, particularly small and medium enterprises (SMEs); a renewed emphasis on raising the extent, quality and relevance of learning in the workplace; effective strategies for responding to critical skills shortages and gaps, bringing together employers, national training organizations and public and private training providers and with an initial focus on IT skills.

National Grid for Learning

Connecting the Learning Society: National Grid for Learning set out the government's plans for creating a national grid for learning.[15] The grid was intended to connect every school in Britain to the information superhighway, with schools connecting to each other and linking to all learning institutions, whether libraries, colleges, universities, museums or galleries. It was planned as a mosaic of interconnecting networks and education services based on the Internet and supporting teaching, learning, training and administration in schools, colleges, universities, libraries, the workplace and homes. Libraries, with their vast stores of information and accessibility to the public, were seen as core to this, making available to all learners, the riches of the world's intellectual, cultural and scientific heritage. The aim is that by 2002 all schools, colleges, universities and libraries and as many community centres as possible will be connected to the Grid. The government intends to take forward the development of the Grid through a nationwide challenge programme and development of an infrastructure of managed services to deliver information and communication technologies to schools, colleges, libraries and other institutions to underpin the Grid. The Grid will be both an architecture (structure) of educationally valuable content on the Internet, and a programme for developing the means to access that content. *Open for Learning, Open for Business: The Government's National Grid for Learning Challenge* (published in 1998) sets out the challenge:

> The Grid will form a key element in helping all of us to identify learning opportunities – linking to the University for Industry and the Public Library Network – and will be a means through which we can participate and contribute to a society in which learning is increasingly accessible and adapted to individual needs.[16]

New Library: the people's network

Complementary to this is *New Library: The People's Network*.[17] Described as a 'defining moment for public libraries', it was the result of a working party set up by the Library and Information Commission to advise government on how public libraries could respond to the challenge of ICT technologies. The report argued for the establishment of a Public Library Networking Agency, which would create the backbone infrastructure and negotiate with library authorities to upgrade their local networks to a common UK standard. *Building the New Library Network*,[18] the implementation report, proposes the development of a new library network which will be initially based on the Internet but which is capable of evolving into a broadband network if required. It suggests that local authorities should purchase kitemarked, managed services based around a core user specification which will vary according to local need. The report put forward a framework for defining, creating and managing the resources available on the network, suggesting that libraries will offer access to educational and cultural material and take on an important new role as creators and developers of digital content. In addition, the report set out a rapid-action programme to equip the nation's librarians with new skills to handle information and communication technology, access databases and online information:

> Easy access to a high performance network will encourage adults to use libraries for self-directed and informal learning and for re-skilling, and will encourage a rapid acceleration in the amount of instructional material made available online. As museums, galleries and other important national collections make their treasures available in digital form, the New Library Network will give easy access to more and more of our cultural heritage. As the government's plans for remotely delivered public services reach fruition and all kinds of official information – including legislation and regulations – are made available in easily searchable electronic databases, libraries will become not just gateways but a key interface between the individual and government at all levels.[19]

The government has committed £50 million for content and £20 million for training of National Lottery money from the New Opportunities Fund. There will also be £6 million made available over the two years 1999–2000 from the Department of Culture, Media and Sport through the Wolfson challenge scheme for infrastructure projects. A press release, issued on 11 March 1999, announced a '£200 million lottery boost for public libraries and lifelong learning', a three-year scheme to help to create a nationwide network of learning centres. This followed the government's announcement in *New Links for the Lottery: Proposals for the New Opportunities Fund*,[20] an initiative to engage more adults in learning at community level and increase community access to ICT by funding a network of centres for community learning, with a particular focus on the socially disadvantaged, people with disabilities and those who would otherwise face significant obstacles to participating in education and training. The initiative was intended to build on the investment in digitization of content and training for teachers and librarians and contribute towards the final phase of building the Public Library Network by providing the infrastructure to make these learning services more widely available.

Networks

What we are beginning to see is a massive investment in networks as an essential element of infrastructure in creating an information society and developing an information economy. This complements the higher education JANET, a highly developed, managed network discussed in Chapter 2. What though such initiatives underline is the need for a coordinated approach across government departments to funding, infrastructure, content creation and training to ensure that conflicting agendas, cultures and languages do not get in the way of the potential presented by a commitment to an information and knowledge society for the future.

The information society

The Library and Information Commission's vision is that the UK will play a leading role in the dominant global information economy through:

- *connectivity*: providing universal access to the products of the human mind
- *content*: creating a digital library of the UK's intellectual heritage of culture and innovation
- *competences*: equipping individuals and organizations to play their full role in a learning and information society.

The Commission's *2020 Vision* recognizes the current challenges facing the information society:[21]

- technology gives the potential for universal access to information and all information becomes potentially available
- access to knowledge/information underpins a democratic society
- information is an international commodity
- knowledge underpins all successful economic activity
- industry is increasingly dependent on an informed workforce
- information must be accessible
- information must be organized and managed
- information skills are fundamental coping skills
- information needs are increasingly complex and may be met from multiple sources
- the discontinuities between technology and our abilities to deal with it need to be understood and managed.

It recognizes that in future, governments, companies and individuals will put a top priority on information and predicts that the UK will be an information/knowledge-based society with the UK acting as a knowledge powerhouse and a hub of the global information economy. Industry and commerce will inevitably become more knowledge-intensive learning organizations. Value-added content and universal connectivity will ensure that every individual will have unfettered access to global information/knowledge. But to access this knowledge, individuals will need a range of literacies to enable them to maximize their potential individually and collectively.

National information policy

In 1997 the Commission issued a discussion document to stimulate debate on the need for a UK-wide national information policy, suggesting that, just as the use of information is all pervasive, the benefits of a national information policy would be felt in all areas of the life of the nation:

- *Education*: an effective IT infrastructure facilitated by a national information policy will further reinforce existing educational structures, as well as facilitate access to alternative lifelong learning opportunities.
- *Citizenship and democracy*: a national information policy would provide a more effective framework for the administration of the United Kingdom at national, regional and local levels.
- *Economic*: a national information policy will act as a catalyst for the widening of access to information, and its effective utilization, in economic and financial planning and market development both at macro and micro level.
- *Community*: an effective national information policy which incorporates a framework for an effective national IT infrastructure can make a significant contribution to the strengthening of communities.
- *Health*: a national information policy which takes particular account of health issues will encourage the development of structures for the provision of up to date information to inform the delivery of effective healthcare.
- *Welfare*: new technologies underpinned by a national information policy will permit the more efficient coordination and delivery of services.
- *Culture and recreation*: a national information policy which would bring in its train a more coordinated approach to the development

of IT-based networks, and telecommunications systems would give encouragement for even greater variety in the provision of cultural and recreational opportunities by both private and public sectors.
* *Legal and regulatory framework*: a national information policy is of particular importance in the light of current developments in data protection, copyright, intellectual property right, legal deposit and personal privacy.[22]

This was discussed from a global perspective in Chapter 1.

The context

This then is the context within which further and higher education operate: an information society where learning for life is increasingly recognized as essential for the individual and the nation. The framework and political climate have already changed and the future will remain dynamic.

The agenda is set for colleges and universities to play a significant role in the learning age, in lifelong learning, in the learning nation or the culture of learning. The opportunity for the whole of society, not merely the rich and privileged, to take advantage of the wealth of information available over networks, will depend heavily on how well this is achieved. Further and higher education will play an increasingly strong and fundamental role in the economic and cultural life of the regions and the nation and the way that both sectors are managed and how they collaborate within the wider community will be crucial to the well-being of all. The effective and efficient management of information will be crucial for these institutions to survive and grow.

Notes

1 Central Office of Information (1998) *Our Information Age: The Government's Vision*. London: Central Office of Information. http://www.number-10.gov.uk
2 Department for Education and Employment (1998) *The Learning Age: A Renaissance for a New Britain*. London: The Stationery Office.
3 Central Office of Information op. cit., pp.1, 7.
4 Department for Education and Employment op. cit., p.7.
5 Ibid., pp.9–10.
6 Ibid., p.10.
7 Ibid., p.13.
8 Ibid., p.47.

 9 Ibid., pp.49–50.
10 Department for Education and Employment (1998) *University for Industry: Engaging People in Learning for Life. Pathfinder prospectus*. London: DfEE. http://www.open.gov.uk/dfee/ufi/index.htm
11 Ibid., p.1.
12 Department for Education and Employment, *The Learning Age*, op. cit., p.27.
13 National Advisory Group for Continuing Education and Lifelong Learning (1997) *Learning for the Twenty-First Century: First Report of the National Advisory Group for Continuing Education and Lifelong Learning* (Fryer Report).
14 Department for Education and Employment (1998) *Towards a National Skills Agenda: First Report of the National Skills Task Force*. London: DfEE.
15 Department for Education and Employment (1997) *Connecting the Learning Society: National Grid for Learning*, the government's consultation paper. London: Department for Education and Employment. http://www.ngfl.gov.uk
16 Department for Education and Employment (1998) *Open for Learning, Open for Business: The Government's National Grid for Learning Challenge*. London: Department for Education and Employment, p.1. http://www.ngfl.gov.uk
17 Library and Information Commission (1997) *New Library: The People's Network*. London: Library and Information Commission.
18 Library and Information Commission (1998) *Building the New Library Network: A Report to Government*. London: Library and Information Commission.
19 Ibid., p.2.
20 (1998) *New Links for the Lottery: Proposals for the New Opportunities Fund* presented to Parliament by the Secretary of State for Culture, Media and Sport by command of Her Majesty, November 1998, Cm 4166.
21 Library and Information Commission (1996) *2020 Vision*. London: Library and Information Commission.
22 Library and Information Commission (1997) Towards a national information policy for the UK: a discussion document. Unpublished committee paper.

3

MANAGEMENT OF INFORMATION IN FURTHER AND HIGHER EDUCATION

Judith Elkin

Colleges and universities in the UK need more than ever before to ensure that information is managed effectively and efficiently. Chapter 2 looked at the current political framework, suggesting that education in the future will be part of a seamless whole, through learning for life within an Information and Learning Age. This then is the climate within which colleges and universities now need to operate. What are the implications and why is the effective and efficient management of information so important?

The Learning Age: a renaissance for a New Britain

The Learning Age emphasized the government's vision of 'a culture of learning' which would help to build a united society, assist in the creation of personal independence, and encourage our creativity and innovation. It also acknowledged our 'superb universities and colleges which help maintain our position as a world leader in technology, finance, design, manufacturing and the creative industries.'[1] One of the key proposals to enable delivery of this vision was to expand further and higher education to provide for an extra 500,000 people by the year 2002.

Further education is highlighted as fundamental to this government vision:

Further education colleges will play a key role in educating both young people and adults. Young people aged between 16 and 18 make up 20 per cent of the four million students in further education. The majority are adults over 18, most of whom study part-time. Student numbers have grown by a quarter in the last four years ... Further education has demonstrated innovation and flexibility in response to new demands from individuals and businesses. Many colleges have worked imaginatively to improve access, operating across a number of sites and working collaboratively with employers, LEAs [local education authorities], community organisations and private training providers. The sector also has an excellent track record in reaching disadvantaged people, helping to reduce social exclusion and promoting employability ... More 16 and 17 year olds study full-time in further education colleges than at school ... The Government endorses the Kennedy report's vision. It sets out a radical vision which we must pursue in the years ahead ... further education will be at the centre of widening participation, together with adult and residential community education and non-traditional approaches.[2]

Higher education (HE), too, is seen as playing a fundamental role in the thrust towards lifelong learning and greater access:

Higher education, offering high quality and high standards, has a central role to play in the Learning Age. It enables young people to complete their initial education up to the highest levels and equips them for work. It provides for an increasing number of mature entrants both as full-time and part-time students. It works with employers to provide them and their employees with the skills they will increasingly need, and with high quality strategic and applied research which benefits both the economy and our national life ... Higher education is a major contributor to local, regional and national economic growth and regeneration.

The Government remains committed to the principle that everyone who has the capability for higher education should have the opportunity to benefit from it ... We wish universities, higher and further education to be beacons of learning in their communities ... Our priority is to reach out and include those who have been under-represented in higher education. They include people with disabilities and young people from semi-skilled or unskilled family backgrounds and from poorer localities.[3]

Further and higher education ▓

Further education

In 1993, further education (FE) was popularly described as the 'Cinderella Sector' but it is now widely expected that further education will be at the heart of lifelong learning. The FE sector consists of 435 colleges supporting different types of study. There are also 52 HEIs delivering further education programmes and 235 'external institutions' which are mainly local authority adult education centres but receive money from the Further Education Funding Council (FEFC). The size range is huge: 27 per cent have fewer than 2000 students while 24 per cent have over 10,000 students. There were nearly 4 million FE students in 1997–8, an increase of 31 per cent since 1994–5, mainly in part-time provision; 15 per cent are on National Vocational Qualification (NVQ) courses, 19 per cent are on General Certificate of Secondary Education (GCSE) or A/AS level courses with the rest on other vocational courses; 3 per cent are on HE programmes. Government plans will add another 420,000 students to the sector; 34 per cent of those whose destinations were recorded progressed from FE to HE.[4]

The FEFC set up a committee, under the chairmanship of Sir Gordon Higginson in July 1993, to advise on measures that it might take to promote the use of technology to enhance the provision of further education. The committee reported that further education needed enabling mechanisms to improve the effectiveness of students' learning, provide better quality information, facilitate the development of new markets and encourage collaboration and reduce duplicated effort. The recommendations were intended to encourage cost-effective, sector-wide developments in the use of technology to promote learning while enabling colleges to tailor facilities, systems and services to match their individual circumstances.[5] The committee also recognized the tremendous changes which had taken place in the further education sector, following incorporation. This had included new funding mechanisms, new data collection introduced by the FEFC and measures designed to enhance the quality of provision, all of which had put new demands on college information systems.

The sector has subsequently invested a substantial amount to improve IT. Most students now have access to good quality computers often in newly developed and well-equipped IT centres. By the time this book is published, a major new investment in IT will have been announced. Current staff development programmes to improve managers' awareness of IT and teachers' basic skills in using IT are already in place, although more support is also needed for the development of external links to ensure that students and staff can gain access to the wealth of material available through the Internet. Colleges need to develop clear strategies which link technology, teaching and learning and staff development.

In terms of management of information, though, inspection reports from the Quality Assessment Council highlight persistent weaknesses in, for example, management information systems. The *Key Skills in Further Education* report from the inspectorate in January 1998 highlighted that:

> an increasing number of colleges are developing an information technology policy. For some it is only a plan for the co-ordination of equipment and computer networks. For others however it is a comprehensive strategy for developing all students' information technology skills.[6]

It looks at developing programmes for key skills in areas like numeracy and IT.

Kennedy Report

The Further Education Funding Council set up the Widening Participation Committee in December 1994, under the chairmanship of Helena Kennedy, QC. Its final report, *Learning Works: Widening Participation in Further Education*,[7] defines further education as 'everything that does not happen in schools or universities': a broad definition which it admits 'misses the mark' of such a 'large and fertile section of the education world.'[8] The report highlights:

> Learning is central to economic success and social cohesion. As we approach the twenty-first century and the immense challenges of the global economy and unprecedented technological change, achieving these inseparable national goals will depend more and more on the knowledge, understanding and skills of the whole population ... Those who are disadvantaged educationally are also disadvantaged economically and socially; equity and viability dictate that all should have the opportunity to succeed. We are convinced that national leadership is required to put learning at the heart of our national common purpose. We must widen participation not simply increase it ... Widening

participation in post-16 learning will create a self-perpetuating learning society.[9]

Underlining the need for widening participation is seen as the need for good quality information, advice and guidance: potential learners need to get information about available opportunities: 'A national entitlement to information, advice and guidance for all should form part of the national strategy for post-16 learning.'[10]

Higher education

Higher education in the UK has changed significantly since the late 1980s. During that time it has more than doubled in size, and the universities and polytechnics have been merged into a single sector with common funding, quality assurance and support systems. Other significant changes have been a major drive to expand and widen participation, a growth in partnership with other agencies, especially further education colleges and employers and a steady growth of work-based learning, including both structured learning in the workplace for full-time students and HE programmes delivered in the workplace to employees. There has been a coordinated national strategy, supported by the Higher Education Funding Councils, to create an extensive technology infrastructure, giving all HEIs a common network and set of services and widespread modularization of the curriculum and growth of credit accumulation and transfer systems which aim to maker it easier for individuals to create individualized programmes to meet their own needs.

British HE still remains a highly devolved system. In England alone, there are 130 diverse HEIs, plus over 70 institutions which offer a combination of further and higher education. Universities and higher education colleges educated 2.8 million students in 1996–7. Less than a quarter were from the group which used to be the mainstay of the old universities – young people studying for a qualification. Of those pursuing a qualification, 64 per cent were mature students and 37 per cent part-timers. Some institutions have over 20,000 students, others fewer than 500; some recruit mainly postgraduate students, while others recruit mainly undergraduates; some recruit only mature entrants, and others recruit only school leavers; some work in a single subject field or profession, while others offer courses and research across a vast range; some have a high proportion of part-time, work-based and distance learning students, others have none.

Dearing Report

A National Committee of Inquiry into Higher Education, under the chairmanship of Sir Ron Dearing, was set up in 1996, to make recommendations on how the purpose, shape, structure, size and funding of higher education, including support for students, should develop to meet the needs of the United Kingdom over the following 20 years, recognizing that higher education embraces teaching, learning, scholarship and research. The title of its report, *Higher Education in the Learning Society*,[11] reflected the vision that informed the report:

> Higher education is fundamental to the social, economic and cultural health of the nation. It will contribute not only through the intellectual development of students and by equipping them for work, but also by adding to the world's store of knowledge and understanding, fostering culture for its own sake, and promoting the values that characterise higher education: respect for evidence; respect for individuals and their views; and the search for truth ... It should, therefore, be a national policy objective to be world class both in learning at all levels and in a range of research of different kinds. In higher education, this aspiration should be realised through a new compact involving institutions and their staff, students, government, employers and society in general. We see the historic boundaries between vocational and academic education breaking down, with increasingly active partnerships between higher education institutions and the worlds of industry, commerce and public service ... Higher education will make a distinctive contribution to the development of a learning society through teaching, scholarship and research.[12]

The need to manage information

With both FE and HE sectors in a period of growth and with a government commitment to widening participation and improving the skills base of the UK, it is clear that the information required to deliver, to record, to monitor, to underpin greater diversity, breadth and depth of education and training, is immense and complex. It will require careful and strategic management. But what does that mean?

Information overload

Reuters Business Information has undertaken a number of independent, international surveys emphasizing the problems of information overload. The objectives of its first survey, which surveyed some 1300 managers in the UK, the USA, Australia, Hong Kong and Singapore, was to investigate: the existence of information overload (perceived or otherwise) within organizations; levels of stress suffered as a result of information overload; the personal cost, the commercial and social implications of information overload. The report, *Dying for Information?*,[13] was published in 1996 and followed up with *Glued to the Screen* in 1997.[14] They show that 'an excess of information is strangling business and causing personnel to suffer mental anguish and physical illness' and use words like 'information junkie' and 'data-holic'. The consequences of this information glut included time-wasting, delaying important business decisions, distraction from job responsibilities, stress, job dissatisfaction, illness and breakdown of personal relationships. In 1996 48 per cent of managers considered themselves victims of information overload. By 1997, that figure had risen to 65 per cent, with 76 per cent of respondents believing that PCs, the Internet and information in general could become addictive, with 53 per cent managers 'craving' information and 54 per cent claiming to get a 'high' when they find the information they have been seeking. However, half the respondents felt unable to handle the amount of information accumulated, 60 per cent believed the cost of gathering the information outweighed its value and 54 per cent worried about making poor decisions, despite the information at their disposal.

Interestingly, two years on, in *Out of the Abyss*,[15] published in late 1998, it appears that information overload is still a major issue on a business and personal level but many people are starting to understand the problem and learning how to cope with it. What appears to be happening around the world is that:

Individuals and businesses are rejecting multiple sources of information in preference to a single source that they believe will actually give them all the information they need. While the quantity of media and content continues to proliferate, a sea-change in the way in which we consume and manage information is becoming perceptible. It is a question of survival of the fittest, because increased financial constraints and the threat of recession mean that companies increasingly require the right information at the right time. Those who learn quickly how to harness the power of information for competitive advantage will set a standard of information management that others will follow. Those who don't will still risk falling into the abyss of stress, confusion and poor productivity.[16]

Out of the Abyss suggests that different countries are at different stages in the information development cycle: eastern Europe at the 'pre-information age' stage, with countries less pressured by time constraints and information overload; Singapore and Hong Kong at the 'middle information age', suffering most from issues relating to information access and factors preventing them accessing the information they really need; western Europe, Japan and the USA entering a new phase in the information age and starting to tackle information overload through the introduction of knowledge management policies or single source strategies that are proving to be effective because they offer people the right information at the right time.

While surveying and commenting on the business community, there are clearly some messages and indeed warnings here for all major institutions and a further demonstration of the pressing need to manage information and consider knowledge management.

Knowledge management

The information society, the information age and the knowledge-based society have become familiar terms since the early 1990s but to date the focus has tended to be on the technology and IT applications, with a concentration on access to that technology and the need to improve skills. Only since the mid-1990s has there been any consideration on the content that flows through the technology – a focus on information and knowledge; how to create it, manage it and use it:

Knowledge is created through accessing, assimilating, sharing and using information. To be really effective in creating knowledge people need to be trained in the necessary information skills . . . Modern communications and information technologies enable access to vast information resources; enable the manipulation, filtering and organisation of relevant information; enable rapid communication and transfer of information; and, if used by an information skills person, can greatly enhance the learning processes and the creation of new knowledge . . . In all walks of life people need information skills as well as computer skills – together they have the potential to create an information society.

Without information skills a computer literate society is likely to be inefficient and frustrated![17]

Knowledge management (KM) has become one of the most discussed management trends of the 1990s. It has caught the imagination of senior executives in many organizations and is seen to have the potential of making those organizations more effective, more creative and more competitive. Through efficiently managing the creation, sharing, capture and utilization of information and knowledge, organizations can leverage their intellectual assets to gain competitive advantage: 'The challenge is to create a culture where knowledge and information are valued and where knowledge creation, sharing and utilization are a natural and instinctive part of business processes.'[18]

Although some people would argue that knowledge cannot be managed, merely facilitated and nurtured, the underlying concepts have considerable benefits for all organizations and considerable potential within the FE and HE sector, although it appears not to have had much impact to date. As Sheila Corrall has suggested:

> KM involves taking a much more holistic view of information, not only combining internal and external information but also co-ordinating planning and control (monitoring) of information, and consolidating informal (soft) and formal (hard) information. KM also requires a strategic focus on valuable knowledge, concentrating on knowledge that will contribute to the improvement of organisational performance . . . So what of KM in HE? Many institutions are already using intranets to manage some types of explicit knowledge, such as minutes of meetings, lecture notes, etc. There is possibly scope for more routemaps and directories, in the form of expert locators and other resource guides, and most HEIs could probably make much better use of the skills of their information professionals if they viewed information holistically and applied the professional expertise of content specialists to managing the wide range of information which underpins institutional operations and decisions – instead of assuming that only academic-related information required that sort of treatment.[19]

Despite the doubts of some information management academics and practitioners, knowledge management is bigger than, and different from, information management. A recent research project to identify the required skills base for knowledge management had the following aims which provide a useful summary:

- to encourage organizations to establish a strategic approach to knowledge management, and to ensure this forms part of the UK national information policy
- to advocate creative applications of knowledge management within organizations
- to disseminate effective techniques for managing knowledge, encouraging good practice
- to establish the roles of people with skills needed to manage knowledge effectively, and the recruitment, training and development activities required.[20]

Joint Information Systems Committee (JISC)

The critical importance of managing information within HE was recognized in the early 1980s through the work of the Computer Board, the body responsible for funding computer provision for UK universities. Initially, the focus of the work was on computing, rather than on information services. Only gradually was a shift made from 'information technology towards information services, from the provision of infrastructure (necessary but not sufficient) to the provision of value added information services.'[21] The Computer Board became the Information Systems Committee (ISC) of the Universities Funding Council in 1991, with a brief which included library and administrative computing. During this time the government was setting up separate higher education funding councils for England, Scotland, Wales and Northern Ireland and incorporating the former polytechnics as new universities. The JISC, a joint body of the HEFCs for England, Scotland and Wales and of the Department of Education Northern Ireland, emerged as a joint committee, to continue the work of the ISC and with a subcommittee, the Information Systems Subcommittee (ISSC) which had a substantial budget line for datasets, funded as part of the core mission. This was the time of setting the principles concerned with content delivery, now largely accepted within the community:

- free at the point of use
- subscription not transaction based
- lowest common denominator
- universality
- commonality of interfaces
- mass instruction.[22]

JISC is charged with providing a network service for the UK Higher Education and Research Councils community, and in this role provides the funding for the development and operation of the network, an activity which is managed by UKERNA. The JISC also provides datasets and other information services, the Electronic Libraries (eLib) programme and a variety of initiatives to encourage and develop use of information systems in the HE sector. JISC acts as a facilitator and enabler – it creates the conditions in which UK HE teaching and research can take maximum advantage of the developments in information technology and information services. This is summed up in its mission statement and Five Year Strategy document:

> To stimulate and enable the cost effective exploitation of informa-tion systems and to provide a high quality national network infrastructure for the UK higher education and research councils communities.
>
> The strength of the Joint Information Systems Committee lies in its ability to provide cohesive services available to all in HE and research, together with the ability to promote and prove innovative, but achievable developments in the exploitation of information systems. It does this by facilitating, not dictating or managing, the use of Information Technology (IT) in the institu-tions. Collaborative advantage has been the key to past successes and is now even more vital as higher education faces unparal-leled financial pressures and an accelerating rate of technological change.[23]

The key elements of the strategy are:

- the provision of more guidance and advice and the raising of awareness, at all levels, of opportunities offered by IS
- a plurality of network provision to meet the diverse needs of the community
- access to a comprehensive and coordinated collection of electronic information
- a tightly focused, modest, programme of innovative developments that will be closely evaluated with widely disseminated outputs.

Thanks to the work of JISC and the commitment of the funding councils, British higher education now has one of the most highly developed systems of access to communication and information tech-nologies in the world. All HE institutions are connected to the JANET/ SuperJANET networks and all academic staff, and most students, have access to the system, and thence to the Internet. JANET pro-vides a model for a managed high quality network development but one currently limited by its terms of reference which prohibit its use for commercial purposes. All HEIs, research council establishments and FE colleges are entitled to primary connection to JANET. This gives them access to the full range of services available on the network. The JISC can allow other bodies to have primary connections if they are primarily engaged in education and research, or if they use the connection only for collaborative research. Currently, JISC takes the view that to extend this service to a wider constituency would jeopardize the primary functions of serving the HE community with scarce and very expensive resources such as the international links: 'The mission will be compromised if the network is expanded to meet the needs of potentially large and very different communities, such as schools, public libraries or the NHS [National Health Service].'[24]

A large part of the UK is now covered by Metropolitan Area Networks (MANs), funded by JISC. MANs provide high bandwidth communications to a wider audience on a regional basis. A MAN aims to serve a geographic area beyond the scope of Local Area Network (LAN) technologies, but is restricted by some well-defined community of interest, often a city and its surroundings. These developments were led by Scotland, where all main HE and FE sites and major research and medical establishments have broadband links capable of carrying high quality live video. The Acceptable Use policies for the MANs tend to be more open than for JANET, for example FaTMAN (Fife and Tayside Metropolitan Area Network) is primarily maintained to support academic and related activities such as teaching, learning and research. This could clearly lend itself to being open for almost any organization to join, and the proposition that public libraries, school libraries and the National Health Service might join is now a distinct possibility.

Regional agenda

The government has committed itself to strengthening regional government, with the setting up of the Scottish Parliament, the Welsh Assembly and regional development agencies for England, shaped by the need to create social, economic and cultural structures that fully exploit the opportunities within the region. The regional development agencies will be working to create regional economies that foster high value-added employment, leading to sustainable long-term economic growth. Regional collaboration between HEIs and between HE and FE institutions has been growing, actively encouraged by the Department for Education and Employment and regional government offices and will be significant in the development and growth of the regions.

Clearly, the argument for bringing together in some way the National Grid for Learning, the University for Industry and the People's Network for Public Libraries through the MANs is a powerful one. Allied to the government's commitment to lifelong learning, which will require access to information from a variety of sources, 'the Government is committed to regionally based policies and the MANs could provide a very elegant realization of a political ambition.'[25]

The role of libraries and information services in the information chain

Central to any consideration of management of information within higher and further education, in addition to management information systems and other areas covered above, must be library and information services. In many ways the discussion above both about information overload and the need to begin to consider knowledge management techniques reinforces the traditional role of libraries in managing information and knowledge. This role is reinforced in an electronic environment. Libraries and information services are managed strategically, locally and cooperatively and offer a range of dynamic, renewable resources, both print and other media. They select, collect and preserve resources, offering a seal of quality and kitemarking and organizing for ready access and use. Library and information services work with knowledge, adding value by evaluating, making accessible, mediating, packaging and promoting information. They are now the learning places of choice for many people, offering an accessible, neutral learning space where people feel secure within a shared value system and a socially inclusive cultural and creative environment, providing catalysts for learning.[26]

Library and information services have a central role to play in managing information for teaching and learning and research, as is demonstrated in the reports below.

Further education

The Scottish Library and Information Council published standards for FE colleges in 1997, *Libraries in Scottish Further Education Colleges*, highlighting the changes that have taken place in the further education sector and pointing out that 'as a core curriculum support service, the quality of the library service reflects the professionalism of the institution as a whole.'[27] It also emphasizes:

the library service is moving sharply into focus as a key to enabling the further development of independent study in the college curriculum. College managers who understand the strategic role of the library service in developing efficient and flexible methods of delivering the curriculum without compromising the quality of education and training will invest in the service.[28]

Higher education

The HEFCs set up a Libraries Review Group in 1992, under the chairmanship of Sir Brian Follett. The report, published in 1993, brought HE libraries and their concerns centre stage.[29] It highlighted the current and changing role and function of the library in the higher education academic environment. It took a positive stance on funding and support within institutions and emphasized the need for strategic planning, cooperation and resource sharing. Its particular influence has been in highlighting the central role of library and information services in the new teaching and learning and electronic environment. The report assumed that:

- all institutions will move to greater operational convergence between their library and information services
- access to networked terminals will be universal
- roles of staff will alter with those currently labelled 'professional' playing a greater role in learner support and academic liaison while other staff provide technical support and enquiry services.

In particular, it led to the establishment of a new subcommittee of JISC, the Follett Implementation Group for Information Technology (FIGIT), and subsequent funding of the Electronic Library programme. This is discussed in Chapter 9 but suffice it to say that, in a relatively short time, it helped the academic community to move rapidly forward in the electronic environment and 'enabled a much wider context for the concept of national digital collections to develop, it provided an R&D stimulus of huge proportions, and it brought together within JISC a much more high profile and rounded view of the information side of the information/technology balance.'[30]

Research Support Libraries Programme

One of the other outcomes from the Libraries Review Group was the development of a national/regional strategy for library provision for researchers, resulting from the Anderson Report (the subgroup of the Follett Committee had been chaired by Michael Anderson). The Research Support Libraries programme is a UK-side programme supported by the four HEFCs to develop and implement the key proposals from the Anderson Report. It comprises both new work and work building on the current funding initiative, specialized research collections in the humanities. The four strands are:

- supporting access to major holdings libraries
- collaborative collection management projects
- support for humanities and social science research collections
- targeted retrospective conversion of catalogues.

A steering group was set up during 1998, chaired by Michael Anderson, to provide strategic management for the development and implementation of the programme and to provide specialist advice to the funding bodies on library and library-related matters; £18.2 million has been committed for grants to institutions under the new programme for the two academic years 1999/2000 and 2000/1.[31]

Cross-sectoral use of libraries

People Flows is a piece of research into cross-sectoral use of libraries,[32] carried out by the Centre for Information Research and Training (CIRT) at the University of Central England in Birmingham and highlighting how individuals use a variety of different libraries for different purposes. It is a particularly pertinent and timely piece of research because it provides real evidence in an area previously served by anecdotal evidence. It reinforces the view that it is essential, when planning for lifelong learning, to ensure that not only should access to learning be seamless but so also should access to resources to support lifelong learners.

Research for the People Flows project began in 1997, as part of the British Library Research and Innovation Centre's Library Cooperation Programme. It arose from a range of concerns around the rapid expansion of the higher and further education sectors, the move towards part-time study and lifelong learning and the knock-on effects this had on the public library sector at a time when public libraries had suffered severe budget cuts and were in real danger of getting left behind in the IT revolution. The focus of People Flows was to investigate the extent of, and the reasons for, the cross-use of publicly funded libraries in two areas of England: Birmingham/

Solihull and Sheffield. The library usage patterns of full-time students had been a major concern for the project right from the start. The research demonstrated that the model of the traditional full-time student was disappearing, as increasingly students were having to work to support their studies or were preferring to study part-time or engage in more flexible, self-directed learning methods. Lifelong Learners emerged as a distinct library user group, with separate patterns of use, cross-use and needs. This group included part-time students and all other respondents who reported being engaged in study at any level, whether for personal interest or in a range of traditional and non-traditional settings. Most lifelong learners using university and college libraries were studying part-time at the institutions where they were surveyed. Lifelong learners surveyed in public libraries, though, were a much more diverse group, including not only people studying for qualifications ranging from NVQs to doctorates but also a large range of people studying in non-formal learning circumstances for a huge variety of purposes.

People Flows showed that there is substantial multi-library use across and within the public, university and college sectors. It also established clearly that the three library sectors surveyed showed different strengths. Public libraries offered a unique geographical spread across the UK, whereas most university libraries offered a far wider range of resources appropriate to study and lifelong learning and college libraries are valued for their easy accessibility and study space. In a climate of lifelong learning, the task on the political agenda is for all three sectors to maximize their strengths for the benefit of all. People Flows argues that addressing cross-use of libraries is as much about accommodating the changing usage patterns of institution's own library users as about opening doors to other potential users and suggests that the solutions raised lie in collaborative and cooperative ways of working.

Summary

This then brings us almost full circle. Further and higher education look set to grow under the New Labour agenda for Lifelong Learning and the Information Society. The framework for growth and change, at the dawn of the twenty-first century, will be dominated by electronic networks which will provide the infrastructure for supporting growth and change. Further and higher education are well set to contribute significantly to the local, regional and national economic and educational agenda and are well placed to provide much of the content and support for learning which will be required for full use of the networks and ensuring that proper links are made to industry, commerce, the public sector, schools and the local community.

Effective and efficient management of information and management of knowledge within further and higher education will become increasingly important to ensure rigorous recording and probity, to support quality delivery of teaching and learning, in whatever media, and to provide a model for a society where lifelong learning can become a reality.

Notes

1 Department for Education and Employment (1998) *The Learning Age: A Renaissance for a New Britain*. London: The Stationery Office, p.10.

2 Ibid., p.47.

3 Ibid., pp.49–50.

4 Further Education Funding Council (1998) *Circular 98/13 Report of the Quality Assessment Committee for 1996/7*. Coventry: FEFC.

5 Further Education Funding Council (1996) *Report of the Learning and Technology Committee* (Higginson Committee). Coventry: FEFC.

6 Further Education Funding Council (1998) *Key Skills in Further Education: Good Practice Report, January 1998* (Report from the Inspectorate), p.16. Coventry: FEFC.

7 H. Kennedy (1997) *Learning Works: Widening Participation in Further Education*. Coventry: FEFC.

8 Ibid., p.1.

9 Ibid., p.15.

10 Ibid., p.89.

11 National Committee of Inquiry into Higher Education (1997) *Higher Education in the Learning Society: Summary Report*. London: HMSO.

12 Ibid., pp.8–9.

13 Reuters Business Information (1996) *Dying for Information? An Investigation into the Effects of Information Overload in the UK and Worldwide*. London: Reuters.

14 Reuters Business Information (1997) *Glued to the Screen: An Investigation into Information Addiction Worldwide*. London: Reuters.

15 Reuters Business Information (1998) *Out of the Abyss: Surviving the Information Age*. London: Reuters.

16 C. Oppenheim (1998) Introduction to *Out of the Abyss: Surviving the Information Age*. London: Reuters, p.2.

17 N. Oxbrow (1998–9) *TFPL Newsletter* 7(winter): 1.

18 TFPL (1999) Skills for knowledge management: building a knowledge economy. London: Library and Information Commission.

19 S. Corrall (1998) Knowledge management: is it our business?, *Ariadne* 18(November). http://www.ariadne.ac.uk

20 Oxbrow op. cit.

21 L. Brindley (1998) The development of JISC strategy on electronic collections. *Library Review*, 47(5/6): 271.

22 D. Law (1997) Atque et valeque: a review of ISSC's work. *JISC News*, 1(spring).

23 JISC (1996) *JISC Five Year Strategy 1996–2001*. Bristol: Joint Information Systems Committee, p.3. http://www.niss.ac.uk/education/jisc/strategy.html

24 JISC Assist (Activities, Services and Special Initiatives Support Team) (1997) Senior Management Briefing Paper, *Janet Connection Policy*, August.

25 Law, op. cit., p.6.

26 Library and Information Commission (1996) *2020 Vision*. London: Library and Information Commission.

27 Scottish Library and Information Council (1997) *Libraries in Scottish Further Education Colleges: Standards for Performance and Resourcing*. Edinburgh: Scottish Library and Information Council and Scottish Library Association, p.2.

28 Ibid., p.7.

29 Higher Education Funding Councils (1993) *Joint Funding Councils' Libraries Review Group: Report* (Follett Report). Bristol: HEFC.

30 Brindley op. cit., p.273.

31 Higher Education Funding Councils (1994) *Joint Funding Councils Libraries Review Report of the Group on a National/Regional Strategy for Library Provision for Researchers*. Bristol: HEFC.

32 People Flows: research carried out for the British Library Research and Innovation Centre. Final report in preparation.

4

INFORMATION STRATEGIES

Ann Hughes

What is an information strategy?

The first question that people tend to ask when contemplating the development of an information strategy is 'What is an information strategy?' There are many definitions around. I suggest the following:

> An Information Strategy encapsulates the institution's policies, practices, procedures and plans with regard to the information requirements and products arising from its Strategic Plan, and the development and exploitation of its information resources and products.[1]

or Elizabeth Orna's:

> Information Strategy is the detailed expression of information policy in terms of objectives, targets and actions to achieve them for a defined period ahead. Information Strategy provides the framework for the management of information.[2]

However, neither of them fully explain what an information strategy actually is. It is very easy to say what it isn't: it is not an information technology strategy, it is not an information systems strategy, it is not an information services strategy. It is quite simply (as James Currall at the University of Glasgow described it) a strategy for information.

The original JISC *Guidelines* described an information strategy as 'a set of attitudes', with some specific attributes, and this phraseology was frequently mocked. However, having worked with information strategies for some considerable time, I am convinced that it is an appropriate description. We are not considering a document (although there is likely to have been one produced somewhere along the line), nor are we just looking at policies (although these may be included). We are looking at the whole way in which information is created, purchased, accessed, managed, exploited and disposed of within the institution. This of course brings with it questions of history and culture within the institution, the way in which people work, and questions of ownership of information.

Purpose

You do not need to know exactly what an information strategy is to begin to develop one: you will find out as the development proceeds. However, what you do need to clarify in your mind is what you wish the information strategy to do for your institution. Why are you developing it? What is the desired outcome? It is only by being clear about this at the outset that you are able to measure your success, or lack of it, later on.

The need for information strategies

During the 1990s, a number of elements came together which prompted an interest in information strategies. First, the resources being expended on IT in higher and further education were growing at an alarming rate. Dearing estimated that the annual expenditure by UK higher education on C&IT was between £800 million and £1 billion, or up to 10 per cent of the total higher education turnover.[3] While this was not necessarily a problem nationally, it was in some institutions. However, there was also a degree of lack of satisfaction with the outcome – it was always the next development which would provide the answers. Coupled with this was the very rapid rate of growth of the sector as a whole, and the feeling that IT should be able to assist institutions in coping with the increasing numbers; with the restricted resources available.

Similar concerns had already been voiced in the commercial world and a number of authors were writing in this area, among them Michael Earl, whose many works cover a range of topics in this field. He takes a broad systems planning approach but also argued against reliance on any one methodology.[4] Approaching this subject from a rather different angle Elizabeth Orna looked at information resource management, and in particular the development of information policies,[5] which she feels must be integrated into the key objectives of the organization. The Follett Report identified the need for a change in the way in which educational institutions planned and provided for their information needs.[6] Although this arose largely from the pressures being placed on institutional libraries due to the increases in student numbers, it relates to the institution as a whole and how the various information services work together. The Hawley Committee Report provided guidelines for boards of directors,[7] which considered information to be an asset to the organization and should therefore be properly identified as such, although not, at that time, in a strict accounting sense. These and other writers brought together the fields of information technology and information science, and initiated the search for an all-embracing information strategy.

This broadening role and changing emphasis from technology to information itself was being mirrored by the higher education committee structure for this area. The Computer Board became the Information Systems Committee in 1991. It had a broader remit than the previous one of academic computing and its membership included library and administrative representation. Consideration of information systems and information management was now on the higher education agenda. This broadening continued when in 1993 the Joint Information Systems Committee was established and set up a subcommittee to develop an Information Systems Strategy framework. Early in its life, the subcommittee dropped the 'Systems' aspect of its title and reinvented itself as a Steering Group. It commissioned Coopers & Lybrand to undertake a study to consider the potential for information strategies within universities and colleges. The initial consultation showed a considerable interest in this area and a more detailed study of what was required was undertaken. The eventual outcome was the original *Guidelines*.[8]

The JISC Guidelines for Developing an Information Strategy

The JISC *Guidelines for Developing an Information Strategy* were published in December 1995 and sent to all HEIs. They outlined the following six-stage process to develop an information strategy:

- *set up*: establishing the mechanisms for developing the strategy, its scope, and gaining top level support
- *context*: identifying the institutional priorities, challenges and opportunities and how the information strategy could help

- *information needs*: identifying the institutional information needs, standards and issues
- *roles and responsibilities*: identifying those with responsibilities for the creation and use of information and what their responsibilities are
- *implementation*: prioritizing and planning projects, encouraging change
- *monitoring and review*: monitoring the effectiveness of the strategy and the contexts in which it operates, reviewing and updating as necessary.

The *Guidelines* received a mixed response, in part because they sought to distance the information strategy from computing and also because of the rather impenetrable way in which they were written. While they gave a feel for what was being suggested, they offered little practical assistance for those tasked with the development of an information strategy within their own institutions. However, they did generate considerable debate and the question of information strategies was the subject of many conferences and meetings with a wide range of delegates. The JISC call for volunteer institutions to pilot the *Guidelines* received a good response and the following six were selected:

- Bath Spa University College (formerly Bath College of Higher Education)
- Queen's University of Belfast
- University of Glamorgan
- University of Glasgow
- University of Hull
- University of North London.

These institutions were selected not only on the basis of the proposals they submitted, but also to represent a range of institutions and regions.

The National Committee of Inquiry into Higher Education (Dearing Report)

The Dearing Committee recommended:

> all higher education institutions in the UK should have in place overarching communications and information strategies by 1999/2000.[9]

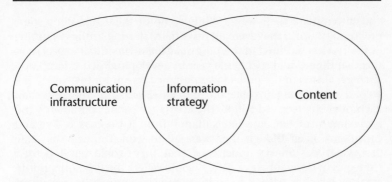

Figure 4.1 Effective use of C&IT
Source: Diagram based on Chart 13.1 Dearing Report

Why did Dearing make this recommendation and what exactly does it mean? Taking the latter part of the question first, there has been considerable debate over the precise meaning of the recommendation and there is certainly inconsistency in the terminology used in the report. However, what is clear is that the recommendation refers to an overarching strategy relating to the overall strategic plan for the institution, embracing competition and collaboration, bringing about change of institutional culture and a rethink of priorities. Throughout the report it is clear that there is a strong belief that 'the innovative exploitation of Communications and Information Technology (C&IT) holds out much promise for improving the quality, flexibility and effectiveness of higher education.'[10] However, there is also the recognition that the provision of the technology is not enough, neither is the additional provision of training in its use, important though this is. The report places the information strategy at the centre, as a means of managing both the infrastructure and the information content, to enable the effective use of communications and information technology: 'The full exploitation of C&IT by higher education institutions in the pursuit of their missions will require senior management to take an imaginative leap.'[11] The information strategy may be seen as a stepping stone to bridge that leap, or a high vantage point from which the leap may more easily be made (Figure 4.1).

Pilot sites

The six pilot sites mentioned above began work on their information strategies in 1996, when a coordinator was appointed to coordinate and disseminate their work. While some of them had done some preliminary work, they were all essentially starting at the beginning of the process outlined in the JISC *Guidelines*. The initial expectation was that they would spend one year in developing their information strategy, although the project was designed to run for two years. The second year would involve the implementation of the strategies. Each pilot site received £5000, the assistance of the coordinator and a maximum of ten days' consultancy from a Coopers & Lybrand consultant. Even though they were all to work through the same process, it was always understood that they would develop their strategies in different ways. These would reflect the differing priority areas which they wished to address, and the different management structures and ethos within the institutions. It is interesting to note a number of these areas and the differences which very quickly became apparent.

Committee structures

Bath Spa (the smallest pilot site) was the exception in using a single-tier committee structure. This had a number of advantages for the smaller institution in that senior staff were more actively involved and resource decisions could often be taken more quickly. However, as the same activities had to be progressed as in the larger institutions, it placed a heavy workload on those senior staff and over time one or two people began to be carrying most of the load.

The other sites all followed the *Guidelines'* suggestion that there should be a two-tier structure, but even here the membership and split of responsibilities varied between the sites. At one extreme there was a considerable overlap of membership which on occasion resulted in debates being repeated by the same people in different committees. At the other extreme there was so little overlap that when the working group (who had made great progress) reported back to the steering group, there was an almost total lack of understanding of what they had been doing. One site found that the perceived conflicts between library services and computing services rendered the initial committee membership unworkable and it was necessary to augment the membership to deflect conflicting views away from individuals and result in a more reasoned debate. At another site, it was found necessary to bring in a very senior member of staff and embed the committee within the formal structure of the institution before great progress could be made.

Priority areas

This is an interesting topic as the initial intentions turned out not to be those which were eventually actioned. Initially there was a broad split between the traditional universities which all said their priority was the administrative and management information, as this was where there were the greatest difficulties. The new universities and HEIs took the view that their main purpose was teaching and learning and that this was where they wished to develop their information strategy. However, in practice, as their strategies developed this broad split became blurred. With the exception of Hull, which did maintain its emphasis on administrative information, the traditional universities took an exemplar or pilot project approach, and examined areas both within teaching and administration (only one in research). On the other hand, the newer institutions, in looking at the process of teaching and learning, discovered that the main problem areas for both students and staff were related to information which might best be described as being at the interface of the teaching and administrative spheres, that is student and resource details. Again Bath Spa was slightly different in that it took a broad overview approach and identified a 'vision' for the institution. It then prioritized which areas to pursue in the implementation projects.

Resources

In these initial stages of the development none of the pilot sites employed additional staff specifically to work on the project, although one did use a consultant who had worked with them before. However, the human resource devoted to the project did vary between sites. Some had no additional specific allocation made and expected staff to develop the information strategy in addition to their already full job descriptions. While enormous strides were made, it is interesting to ponder what might have been achieved had some additional resource been available. It is also fair to say that by the end of two years, enthusiasm was beginning to wane and efforts were being made to pass on responsibility for the development to others.

The Queen's University of Belfast utilized postgraduate students to undertake much of the work. While this was successful in that they produced good results, the students did require rather more supervision than had been anticipated. However, where students within the institution require project work in this area, they can produce good results and they benefit from working on 'real' projects. The supervision required can therefore be offset against the problems of finding suitable projects elsewhere.

Hull was fortunate in that following a reorganization it had available two posts which were reinvented as information managers. Other approaches were to allocate a proportion of one or two people's time to this area of work. They would coordinate the activities of the committee(s) although part of the work would be undertaken by committee members and enthusiasts. An alternative approach was to utilize other initiatives, which were already taking place within the institution. The information strategy could provide some support and steer to these initiatives, and seek to ensure that they achieved the aims of the information strategy, but built on the work already done or at least budgeted for.

Implementation projects

A wide range of implementation projects is being undertaken. These include the gradual rolling out of new processes and systems relating to corporate information; the development of a new medical curriculum; an investigation into knowledge management; the development of on-line reading lists; and the development of a staff development pack.

Findings

The experiences of the pilot sites are described in the case studies which informed the development of, and are included as part of, the new guidelines, *Guidelines for Developing an Information Strategy – the Sequel*. They also influenced the way in which the *Guidelines* are presented. Institutions or individuals requiring specific guidance on the process of developing an information strategy are advised to consult these.

The major findings from the pilot sites are summarized below:

• In broad outline, the process described in the original *Guidelines* did work. However, a number of changes were required to simplify the process and take into account variations between institutions.
• With regard to the various stages originally outlined, it was found that a number could be merged and/or reordered. In particular the first two stages were merged as the activities described did not have to be undertaken sequentially. However, it is still stressed that these stages are absolutely crucial to the development and

cannot be skipped over. In fact a number of the pilots had to return to the early stages to clearly identify the priorities for the institution. It comes down to this question of identifying what the information strategy is intended to achieve, this in turn hinges on the mission of the institution. As Michael E. Porter identifies in 'What is strategy?', the role of leadership is essential.[12] This is corroborated in the importance that has been found to be crucial, of there being top-level support for the information strategy. Without a clear idea of what the institution is trying to achieve, it is difficult (if not impossible) to develop an effective information strategy.

- External consultants were found to be of limited help. The exception to this was where a consultant already had an intimate knowledge of the institution and a full understanding of the higher education environment. Where details were to be obtained from senior staff, they did seem to talk more openly to an outsider. In addition, the consultant could ask the 'stupid questions' which would not be raised by those encumbered with the 'baggage' of the institution.

- The original *Guidelines* suggested that the identification of information needs required a considerable amount of detail gathering for all information items. In practice, none of the pilot sites went down to this level of detail. While the details may well be required in areas in which there are problems, there is no point in collecting it if everything is all right. In other words take the view that 'if it ain't broke, don't mend it'.

- Finally, it was found that institutions actually welcomed far more direct guidance than had previously been thought. The original *Guidelines* were felt to be a good awareness-raising document, but failed to tell them what to do. The new document therefore was more prescriptive, while still recognizing that the activities outlined were just suggestions. It was always stressed that where an institution already had experience of an alternative approach, this could still be utilized.

Pilot site benefits

The pilot sites are all continuing with their information strategy development, even though there is now no funding for it from JISC. They must therefore feel it is beneficial. It is acknowledged that it is difficult to quantify the benefits from this approach, and this is an area on which further work is required. However, what is evident from the pilot sites is that the information strategy committee provides a unique forum within the institution for information matters to be considered. It brings the issues considered and the decisions taken to the attention of a wider constituency, and those decisions have more credibility throughout the institution. In summary, the pilot sites are seeing a gradual change of attitude and culture within the institution.

New developments

The new *Guidelines* which incorporated these changes were published in April 1998. Along with them was a circular calling for proposals for a further wave of what were termed 'exemplar sites'. Again a range of institutional types was required and those selected reflect varying stages of development with regard to information strategies. The intention is that these sites, coupled with the original pilot sites, will provide a base of experience which will be available to the whole HE community to augment that of the coordinator. Twenty-three institutions submitted proposals, from which the following were selected:

* Birkbeck College, London
* University of Leeds
* University of Northumbria at Newcastle
* The Open University
* Roehampton Institute, London
* Staffordshire University
* University of Strathclyde
* University College Worcester
* University College Writtle, Chelmsford.

In view of the experiences of the original pilot sites, these institutions are all required to devote a minimum of a half-time post to the development of the information strategy. They again have been allocated a minimal level of resource from JISC, and have the benefit of advice and assistance from the coordinator. Let us now look at each of them in turn.

Birkbeck College, London

Although an information strategy statement was drafted in 1995/6, this was only a statement of general principles and not a strategy document intended to generate specific actions within stated timescales. The need for a 'detailed information strategy' was identified as a task for completion in the current planning period by the college's strategic plan (1996/7–2000/1). A new master, Professor Tim O'Shea, took up his post in January 1998 and reviewed the college's strategic direction and priorities. This provided an ideal opportunity to review the previous information strategy work and develop it in line with the new priorities. The maximization of student numbers was identified as the single most important challenge facing the college. Work began on a new information strategy in the autumn term 1998 by a committee established by the college's new pro-vice-master for communications and information technology. The college is adopting a 'vision' approach to the information strategy to prioritize areas for specific attention. Particular attention will be paid to student information needs and as far as possible delivering information directly to students. As an information strategy is concerned with changing attitudes, staff development will be a key element of the strategy.

University of Leeds

While work on the development of an information strategy commenced some time ago, it was originally concerned only with the areas of teaching and learning. In 1997, this brief was extended to enable the information strategy to take a more holistic view of the institution. Committee structures and staff are in place and the beginnings of a strategy have been incorporated formally in the university's corporate plan. In such a large and diverse institution, many projects and initiatives are always in hand, many of which relate directly to information. The approach adopted is therefore to build on some of these initiatives, to learn from them, and ensure that they really do meet the institution's information needs. Specific projects have yet to be selected, but it is hoped to include areas of both academic and administrative information.

University of Northumbria at Newcastle

The university's commitment to an information strategy goes back to 1993, when the university executive adopted a vision of gradually more information being delivered through the same electronic channels and being a key resource for the university. At the same time the computing and library departments were brought together as a powerful focus for information developments. A formal information strategy document was approved in 1995, followed by a second edition in 1997. The university now envisages the development of effectively an additional 'Global Electronic Campus' to which any member of the university has equal access. However, much of the current work is focused on the development of a 'business case' approach to information decisions and a standard methodology for projects. This work is being led by a full-time information strategy manager.

The Open University

The university has no information strategy *per se*, but there already exist a number of components that might be embraced by a developed information strategy. Examples are Open University strategies for course materials development and production, for learning technology development and teaching, for library services and for information systems. The last has largely been used to engineer process change and to address information needs in the non-academic activities of the university, but far less so in respect of the core academic activities of research, curriculum development and course production methods. These are areas which will be considered within the plans to develop an information strategy. The initial pilot project will examine three faculties' plans. Its objectives include the investigation of the internal and external information needs of strategic planners and strategy implementers, some with experience of knowledge management applications, one with none. In addition gaps in information sources will be identified and attitudes towards the unit plans and the use made of them investigated. The results will be used as the basis for planning more focused information strategy work, with which will be integrated information systems strategy work focusing on the corporate direction, planning, management, business analysis and market planning functions.

Roehampton Institute, London

The development of an information strategy began in 1996/7 when an information strategy working group was established. Most of the first two stages of the development have already been achieved and the institute's strategic plan includes in its operational objectives the development and implementation of an information strategy. Current priority areas for investigation include the cultural changes required for information sharing; staff and student development needs in C&IT; development of an information policy; and informal communication requirements and solutions.

Staffordshire University

During 1996, the university began a series of initiatives that might best be described as 'business process re-engineering'. Under the banners of Process Improvement Programme (PIP) and Building a Learning Community (BLC), all the main administrative, management and learning processes across the university were targeted for systematic, strategic review. Taken together, these provided much of the information audit required within an information strategy. Together with ongoing information technology strategy, human resource strategy and estates strategy developments, a picture emerged of the overall information flows, needs and potential blockages in the university's key information processes. A steering group was formed to bring all these strands together into an integrated information strategy. The implementation phase has commenced with two complementary strands: internal, to ensure that the systems and strategies are soundly based and robust; external, to create the external partnerships and linkages that will take the region forward.

University of Strathclyde

The university has been actively involved in the development of an information strategy since 1995. This now covers all areas of activity: teaching and learning, research, management and administration, business and consultancy. Current areas of implementation include projects on new teaching methods and modes of study, intranet-based campus wide information systems, intelligent Web worlds to support the Strathclyde research community, virtual universities to address various educational opportunities, and digital libraries. One of the main priority areas will be to consider the effectiveness of the university's use of C&IT, to perform cost/benefit analysis calculations for new investments and to assess return on investment from extant infrastructure and services.

University College Worcester

Work started on the development of an information strategy in 1996. A Phase I report was produced in June 1997 which identified

key frameworks for the development of the institutional information strategy, key information groups within the college, information objectives, methodologies for detailed development of strategies
within all areas of the college, and recommendations for action.
Phase II includes the monitoring of the implementation projects
arising from the earlier recommendations and the development of
analyses in particular aspects of two key areas: learning and teaching,
and administrative systems. There is a strong need and desire to extend
consultation with partner institutions, especially in respect of student and course information. In addition there is a need to broaden
participation in the information strategy across the institution even
further. These form the two main themes for current work.

University College Writtle, Chelmsford

The development of the information strategy is in its early stages. A
questionnaire has been distributed to assess the present position and
future expectations of staff and students with regard to information
needs. While priority areas are not yet finalized it seems likely that
significant emphasis will be placed on the cultural changes required
to embrace new learning techniques and utilize emerging technologies effectively.

Where now for the JISC Information Strategies Initiative?

As can be seen above, the exemplar sites are at various stages of the
development of the information strategy and provide a range of
opportunities for the community as a whole to learn from their
experiences. Many institutions do experience difficulties with the
development of an information strategy. The coordinator, assisted
by representatives of the pilot and exemplar sites, is available to
help institutions in this work. In more general terms the experiences
of the selected institutions are also available through conferences,
publications and on the Web, for others to learn from.

Evaluation

An evaluation of the initiative,[13] undertaken early in 1998, raised a
number of issues which could form a framework for the ongoing
evaluation of this work. Some of these reflect some of the early

concerns regarding information strategies which it appears cause resistance to their development. One of these relates to a feel that information strategies encourage standardization and centralization, as opposed to diversity and academic individualism. This certainly does not have to be the case. While an information strategy would look for efficiency, and it is clearly inefficient to duplicate tasks unnecessarily, it would also seek effectiveness. Where there are good reasons for diversity, these should be acknowledged by the information strategy. What the information strategy provides is a forum in which these issues may be discussed and considered, and decisions taken openly as to the best way forward for the institution as a whole.

Another misconception is that the development of an information strategy will inevitably lead to convergence (or merger) of the information services. This is certainly not the case as the pilot sites exhibit a range of service structures. Indeed it may even be that the contrary is the case, in that the information strategy provides a forum where the various information service areas will be represented and can consult with each other. There does need to be understanding and cooperation between them, but this can be achieved in many ways.

A further point of resistance was the view that the original *Guidelines* sought to exclude colleagues from computing services from this process. While this was certainly not the intention, it was recommended that the development should not be led from within that service. The reason for this was to emphasize the leading role of 'information'. The institution needed to understand that this was not a strategy about computing, it involved the core business of the institution. However, the involvement of staff within computing was required. In practice some institutions have successfully placed the development of their information strategy within the computing section. What is required is that the emphasis is on the information itself, that all areas of the institution are involved, and that those driving the strategy are able to relate it to the main business of the institution. It requires champions who can talk about the benefits to the institution, and its members, not about the technicalities of how those might be achieved.

The future?

Few, if any, educational institutions have a mature information strategy of the type recommended by the *Guidelines*. So there is much work still to be done. However, the commercial sector, and increasingly institutions, are moving on to the concept of knowledge management. In many aspects it shares much of the information strategy ethos. In his Preface to the original *Guidelines*, Sir John Arbuthnott describes information as 'the lifeblood of the institution', and education, along with quite a number of commercial concerns, has been described, or described itself, as an 'information business'.[14] However, perhaps 'knowledge business' is more appropriate?

The current literature on knowledge management relates mainly to the commercial sector. Knowledge management has been defined as 'the collection of processes that govern the creation, dissemination, and utilization of knowledge to fulfil organizational objectives'.[15] It also acknowledges the fact that people and attitudes are the key to effective knowledge management. Overwhelmingly the reason given as to why they felt knowledge was important was 'to gain competitive advantage'.[16] Surely this is what institutions require to be successful in 'the nascent world market for higher education'.[17]

Notes

1 Joint Information Systems Committee (unpublished) *Guidelines for Developing an Information Strategy – The Sequel*. Nottingham: JISC.
2 E. Orna (1990) *Practical Information Policies*. London: Gower, p.19.
3 National Committee of Inquiry into Higher Education (1997) *Higher Education in the Learning Society* (Dearing Report). London: HMSO.
4 M.J. Earl (1992) *Strategic Information Systems Planning: The Contribution of Formal Methods*, management working paper no. 92/7. London: London Business School Centre for Research in Information.
5 Orna op. cit.
6 Higher Education Funding Councils (1993) *Joint Funding Councils' Library Review Group: Report* (Follett Report). Bristol: HEFC.
7 Klynveld Peak Marwick Goerdeler (KPMG) (1995) *Information as an Asset: The Board Agenda* (Chairman Dr Robert Hawley), KPMG Impact Programme.
8 Joint Information Systems Committee (1995) *Guidelines for Developing an Information Strategy*. Bristol: JISC.
9 National Committee of Inquiry into Higher Education op. cit., p.206.
10 Ibid., p.202.
11 Ibid., p.205.
12 M.E. Porter (1996) What is strategy?, *Harvard Business Review*, November–December: 61–78.
13 S. Kushner and N. Norris (1998) *Evaluation and the JISC Information Strategies Programme*. Norwich: Centre for Applied Research in Education (CARE).
14 Joint Information Systems Committee (1995) op. cit., p.2.
15 P. Murray and A. Myers (1997) The facts about knowledge, *Information Strategy*, September: 29–33.
16 Ibid., p.29.
17 National Committee of Inquiry into Higher Education op. cit., p.204.

5

THE ADMINISTRATOR AND INFORMATION

John O'Donovan

'Information, information, information' is not an election winner, but is the sustenance of university life and meat and drink to the administrator. Collecting, organizing, analysing and disseminating information is essential for good management and decision making. The support of administrators is vital to this provision. This chapter explores this role, providing a framework of ideas, concepts, views, practical tips and advice that can be brought to bear on the day-to-day activities of administrators. Much of what is here has a sound theoretical base, but the chapter will also draw your attention to the realities of working in people-intensive organizations, where information management theory can appear artificial and sterile. It is not intended for information specialists nor as a detailed 'how to' manual since many excellent texts and papers already exist, such as those by Maddison,[1] Pellow,[2] or the JISC Technology Applications Programme (JTAP) reports published by the Joint Information Systems Committee.[3]

Information strategies

Planning for the delivery of information, for research, teaching, and management should emerge from the development of an information strategy (IS), which in turn should be directly linked to the institution's main business (that is academic) strategy. The development of information strategies is discussed in Chapter 4 in this volume but the claims made for the state of development of information strategies should be regarded with some scepticism. The Standing Conference of National and University Libraries (SCONUL) published a series of working papers in 1994, where Meadows and Hopkins stated that 21 per cent of the universities surveyed already had information strategies and another 44 per cent were in the process of development.[4] This would appear to be a reasonably healthy situation yet, if true, why did the UK funding councils feel it necessary to promote a national initiative to encourage universities to develop ISs? Where such strategies exist they are more likely to be IT or information systems strategies, shelfware which has little relevance for the institution, or information strategies in the very early stages of development. The national initiative referred to above began in mid-1994. A set of *Guidelines*, first produced in 1995,[5] was revised and published together with six case studies in 1998.[6] In the past such national initiatives have not proved a great success and as Allen and Wilson point out,[7] in their discussion of a coherent model for an information strategy, JISC has no authority to enforce information strategies; there does not appear to be any significant funding attached to the information strategies, and perhaps more importantly 'a simple minded transfer of experience in strategic information planning from the private sector to universities, will not serve the goals of the institutions'.[8] They further argue that the top-down, rational approaches adopted from business are likely to fail because they ignore the political nature of universities. This may have some credence but most large organizations have to cope with internal politics. Perhaps a major reason for the highly political nature of universities is the lack of clear strategies. After all in the absence of institutional goals, private agendas will grow to fill the vacuum.

Information systems development

The JISC Information Strategy Initiative already resembles another major information related national UK project, the Management and Administrative Computing (MAC) Initiative. This aimed to improve the standard of information systems in higher education and was started by the UK University Grants Committee (the predecessor of the funding councils) in 1988. The basic concept was to design a blueprint of core information needs which was broken down into six major applications. Universities were eventually organized into four cooperative families, formed around a common software development environment. Until independent and thorough research is carried out and published, the true cost and achievements of this initiative will not be known. It is clear from informal networks and the experience of others that this project lost its way some time ago. Some universities pulled out completely, some have gone back to basics and started again, whilst others are still attempting to implement systems which derive from their original 'MAC Objectives'.

Whether undertaking a large-scale project such as the MAC Initiative, or a smaller scale project such as the establishment of a local student registration system, both empirical and theoretical studies point to the following good practice for systems development:

• Ensure that the appropriate level of management is fully committed to the project (for example, if it is an institution wide project then there should be clear and active commitment from the president or vice-chancellor).
• Ensure that there is a detailed project plan with clear aims and objectives, showing the individual tasks and how they link, the resources needed, with milestones and timescales clearly identified.
• Resource the project properly, that is do not simply add the work to already overloaded staff.
• Take care to ensure that the user community is properly identified (to include secretarial and clerical staff who often have to make the systems work on a day-to-day basis) and remember that most administrators are there to serve the whole institution and do not just work for 'the centre'.
• Carry out a thorough user needs analysis to include data flow diagrams and activity flow analyses.
• Analyse the current system (whether paper based or IT based) to see if, in the first instance, improvements can be achieved simply by changing current procedures.
• Ensure that the complexity of the project is not underestimated (for example it is commonly believed that it is an easy matter to produce teaching timetables automatically, but this requires linking degree choices, module choices, regulations, physical asset registers, availability of temporary and permanent teaching staff and so on, all of which makes for an enormously complex task).
• Create a culture of risk taking, being prepared to accept failure and to pull the plug if the project is clearly not going according to plan.
• Choose the best possible people for the role of project manager and project team members. If necessary they should be seconded from other parts of the administration or office. The project manager must have excellent people management, organizational and analytical skills and be prepared to take hard decisions. It can be useful to include one or two sceptics in the team but be warned that you will soon tire of the type who sees everything as a problem.

- Provide appropriate training especially in formal project management techniques.
- Ensure that enthusiasm and momentum can be harnessed and established early on in the project through some small successes.
- Keep the 'techies' at bay until the last possible moment otherwise they will take over and provide a solution somewhere short of the ideal.
- Be prepared to learn from other parts of the institution and from other institutions in both the public and private sectors – do not reinvent the wheel.
- Consider collaboration with other HEIs, although Fielden,[9] from an analysis of projects in the Commonwealth, argues that the scope for collaboration is limited to software development only under very tightly controlled circumstances; consortia for evaluating commercial packages and negotiating procurements; sharing consultancy support in implementation or shared project management; or partnerships where the numbers are kept small (at most four) and where the partners have similar missions and cultures.
- Be prepared to purchase 'off the shelf' systems and to accept that an IT-based system (whether in-house or bought-in) may not be able to deliver 100 per cent of your needs.

Data and information

Administrators add value through the transformation of data into useful information. This role is present in almost every administrative task at every level in the organization, for example, listening to committees and transforming what they say into a meaningful record of the discussion (operational level); analysing tables of competitive data with summaries, commentary and analysis to benchmark the performance of the university and its departments (tactical level); analysing softer information, such as government policy, to provide senior management with overviews of changes to the external environment that may affect strategic plans (strategic level).

The common theme of these examples is that they are all part of decision-making processes at different levels of the organization. Information is an important resource and its handling should not be wasteful. Yet how familiar are experiences such as committees asking for analyses of information then showing no interest when provided at the next meeting; senior managers asking for as much detail as those in operational roles; information requested simply because it appears interesting; requests for the same analyses from different parts of the organization; levels of precision being demanded which take little account of underlying assumptions and how changes in the magnitude of dependent variables may affect the outcome; lack of knowledge of who owns information, what information is available, where it is stored, and how to access it; last minute requests for information which deflect resource from more important tasks.

These examples show the need for information to be managed properly, and to ensure that it is organized, planned, used, controlled and disposed of according to the criteria set out in an information management policy. Such a policy should derive from the institutional information strategy but this is not a necessary precondition to the development of good practice which, as Sangway has shown,[10] could include the following elements:

- Management information needs are made clear at the outset of the development of any policy or plan.
- The information must be relevant to the need, with those staff responsible for the information support being allowed (no matter how junior) to question that the information needed is fit for the purpose intended.
- The costs of providing information should be made explicit and recharged to the 'customer' with premiums added for last minute requests for information.
- All management information belongs to the institution and should be available to all those who have a legitimate need, subject to any legal considerations.
- Manage by exception through the establishment of standards and performance indicators to avoid the 'need all the detail' syndrome.
- Eliminate duplication by ensuring that all information providers are aware of what management information and reports exist.
- Ensure that information is retained for the minimum length of time commensurate with legal, historical and technical needs and provide for the systematic and planned destruction of all information not scheduled for permanent retention.
- Where non-current information must be retained it should be stored according to a uniform structure and in the most effective manner (for example off-site and off-line).
- Clarify ownership of information, that is identify those who have responsibility for adding value and those who are responsible for the collection, maintenance, and quality of the data.

The application of such guidelines can then drive the development of a systems plan where a thorough analysis is undertaken of current practices, procedures, activities, and information flows to improve information management.

Competive analysis ▪

Universities and colleges are working in an increasingly competitive environment and this has meant a growth in the use of data (such as Higher Education Statistics Agency (HESA), OECD) that allows institutions to compare themselves with similar organizations. Administrators add value to such data through quantitative and qualitative analysis. When using such information it is important to note the following:

* Categorization varies between universities and colleges and between the institutions and the bodies requesting the data.
* Different sources of the same data are often incompatible.
* Formatting of data often varies so that combining different data items to produce more sophisticated analyses can be very time consuming.
* Statistical publications can be produced months or even years late.
* Changes to requirements and formats make comparability between years problematic.

League tables

Many managers and administrators will be familiar with that virulent condition LTP (league table panic) which overcomes senior executives in universities and colleges once or twice per year. The only known cure is the sudden diversion of significant administrative resource to determining why the performance is so depressing and then spinning this to assure everyone else that this is really good news. The producers of these tables argue that they are simply fulfilling a need that has been generated by growth in the system, which creates far more choice, and a corresponding growth in consumerism and demand for value for money services.

Nevertheless there is considerable controversy surrounding their publication and use. The most frequent criticisms are that the tables attract a significance beyond their worth, especially overseas where they enjoy an implied authority because of the publications in which they appear; the tables are too simplistic to satisfy the varied needs of potential students; the measures included are often arbitrary, the scaling and/or weighting of the measures is arbitrary, the accuracy of the data is questionable, the data are easy to manipulate in ways that were not intended, and dependent measures are used despite being added together to create a total score; comparatively simple tables cannot represent the complex inputs, processes and outputs of teaching and research; the tables do not compare like with like and take no account of institutional mission.

However, it is important to bear a number of points in mind, namely that the producers of these tables are aware of the criticisms and are collaborating with the HE sector to improve the quality of the information; that the audience (primarily prospective students) is sophisticated and takes much more into account than just the tables; that other sectors (schools, health services, local government) use league tables leaving little case for tertiary education to be excluded; no matter how the data are grouped, producers claim that the tables are fairly robust under a wide range of measures and weights; these tables are derived from information provided by the institutions themselves or by other official bodies.

It is clear that tables are here to stay, which means that it is in the interests of the sector to work as closely as possible with the commercial providers to guarantee the best possible product. As Morrison *et al.* point out, the measurement literature offers institutions the opportunity to demand that instruments claiming to compare them should be capable of meeting minimum standards of reliability and validity.[11]

Whether this is feasible will depend on the extent of cooperation between institutions, and as Wagner argued,[12] the tensions created by these tables can often reflect the differences within the sector. Some believe there exists a cultural bias whereby research led institutions are seen as superior rather than of equal value to teaching led institutions. Yorke argues that this finds its way into the choice of indicators used in the tables as they are dominated by the research function.[13] Although there may have been some undervaluation of teaching in the past this has been corrected and teaching now receives a high weight. Perhaps we could do worse than copy the American approach used by *US News and World Report*, where the providers display their information according to four categories of institution which are determined independently of the league table provider.[14] This would go some way to answering those who argue that mission is not taken into account. Cooperation on more technical aspects could introduce trend analysis, increase cross-checking to ensure consistency, and ensure that an agreed measure of added value is included. The latter suggestion is likely to cause as much argument as the tables themselves and whether it can be achieved is doubtful.

It has already been pointed out that the tables are based mainly on data supplied by the HE and FE sectors, so that much of this information is already available publicly and in electronic format.

Therefore the long-term solution may lie with information technology. The sectors have the national mechanism and resource to develop user friendly software that would allow this information to be accessed across the World Wide Web (WWW) in schools, libraries, businesses and even in the home, enabling users to combine the data in whatever way they wished.

Training for information ■

Training is essential to ensure that administrative staff have the right skills and knowledge to perform tasks effectively. It must be carefully planned and continuously reviewed. It must be closely tied to the needs of the organization and budgeted for from the outset. The skills required will vary considerably depending on the particular role of the administrator.

Statistics

Many administrators will at some stage in their career be involved with quantitative measurement and control. However, it is not uncommon to find administrators who are 'number blind' and cannot, for example, see the inconsistent value in a dataset or use averages without any appreciation of the importance of the spread of values. This feel for numbers is essential for the purposes of data handling and analysis. For example, we need to understand the magnitude of numbers, how they may change with time, how they behave collectively, understand the limitations to precision and accuracy, and understand the relationships between different sets of numbers. In the UK this type of training, especially for those with a non-scientific background, is either neglected or provided at a very basic level. Such training could cover descriptive statistics (such as measures of averages and dispersion), how to summarize and present data, probability and probability distributions, statistical inference, relationship between two or more variables, mathematical modelling and so on.

Communication and information technology

So far there has been deliberately limited mention of information technology, yet gaining access to data, distributing data, storing data, and modifying and manipulating data have been transformed as the result of advances in C&IT. Training in the use of PCs and standard packages (word processing or spreadsheets) is now routine in most universities and colleges. However, it is difficult to imagine carrying out day-to-day duties without the knowledge and skills required to make use of the Internet and intranets which, since the early 1990s, have revolutionized the lives of administrators. The use of email is now routine and, from a simple messaging facility, it has grown into a fundamental tool for both internal (the speed at which draft documents can be discussed, finalized and circulated rapidly to large numbers of individuals has been improved dramatically) and external communication allowing good practice to be shared nationally and internationally.

The WWW is now the most popular way of accessing information over the Internet and the growth in usage within administration has been phenomenal since the mid-1990s. The WWW is the gateway to a huge number of multimedia information sources and services across the globe so that training in its use is essential. It can provide access to:

- electronic journals and newspapers (to write this chapter I accessed an electronic management journal, the *Financial Times* and the US News site in the USA)
- the information resources of private and public organizations including other HEIs and government sources
- bibliographic services which allow large number of publications to be searched for relevant references and publications
- library catalogues
- professional administrators' groups
- educational statistics.

The range of services is vast so that training needs to focus on the most effective ways to find the information that is needed. Most universities and colleges now provide this type of training for their own staff.

Awareness training

Such is its significance that IT developments need the constant attention of administrators at all levels. New possibilities are emerging all the time which can improve the effectiveness of business processes. The formal approach of defining needs and then developing or buying in the software is fine in theory, but it is not easy to imagine the benefits of, for example, electronic scheduling software or the benefits of document management systems or the application of Lotus Notes to university administration without seeing these in working situations. Clearly it is in the interest of universities and colleges to develop administrator's awareness of C&IT, yet it is not clear that this has been tackled successfully in a structured way within the UK. For example very few administrators are aware of the JISC Technology Applications Reports, casting doubt on the success of this initiative. C&IT awareness is still too often left to word of mouth or chance encounters with colleagues from other fields. There are considerable formal and coordinated approaches to the use of C&IT in teaching and learning and the development of the electronic library, but a similar level of effort has not been directed towards the development of the 'electronic office'.

Data protection

The Data Protection Act 1984 regulates the use of automatically processed personal information, that is information which is processed on computer technology and is about living, identifiable individuals. This information need not be particularly sensitive and can be as little as a name and address.

Registered data users must comply with the Data Protection Principles. Broadly they state that personal data shall be

- obtained and processed fairly and lawfully
- held only for lawful purposes which are described in the register entry
- used or disclosed only for those or compatible purposes
- adequate, relevant and not excessive in relation to the purpose for which they are held
- accurate and, where necessary, kept up to date
- held no longer than is necessary for the purpose for which they are held
- able to allow individuals to access information held about them and where appropriate correct or erase it
- surrounded by proper security.

There are some exemptions: registration may not be necessary where personal data are

- held in connection only with personal, family or household affairs or for recreational use

- used only for calculating wages and pensions, keeping accounts, or keeping records of purchases and sales solely for accounting purposes
- used only for distributing articles or information
- held by a sports or recreational club which is not a limited company
- required by law to be made public
- exempt to safeguard national security
- used only for preparing the text of documents.

The Act established the Office of the Data Protection Registrar, the duties of which include maintaining a register of data users and computer bureaux and making it publicly available; disseminating information on the Act and how it works; promote compliance with the Data Protection Principles; encourage the development of Codes of Practice to help data users to comply with the Principles; considering complaints about breaches of the Principles or the Act.

Failure to comply is a criminal offence. If the Data Protection Registrar considers that breaches of the principles have taken place then enforcement action can be taken against the data user, who may appeal to an independent tribunal.

EU Data Protection Directive

This took effect from 24 October 1998, and the Act will be brought into force from 1 March 2000. At least 80 per cent of compliance with the new Act flows from complying with the 1984 Act. In many areas detailed advice about compliance will need to be drawn from practical experience in interpreting the provisions of the new Act. There will be a three-year transition period for data protection officers (DPOs, who are the administrators normally responsible for ensuring compliance with the Act) to bring processing already underway into compliance with the new law, and data already held in manual filing systems need not comply with many aspects of the new law until 2007.

Major differences

The new Act allows enforcement against those who are exempt from notification. DPOs will therefore need to consider how to comply with the new law even if exempt from the requirement to notify. DPOs will have to make public on request the details of their processing, but until the notification regulations have been published there is very little DPOs can do to review their registration requirements under the new law.

The new Act expressly provides certain conditions which must be met for personal data to be treated as processed fairly. Stricter conditions apply to the processing of 'sensitive data', for example information on racial or ethnic origin, political opinions, religious or other beliefs, health, sex life and criminal convictions. The consent of the individual will usually have to be obtained before sensitive data can be processed. The new Act states explicitly what security precautions data users must take and DPOs should ensure that existing security measures are appropriate for the types of data that are being processed.

Data subjects are also entitled to a description of the data being processed, a description of the purposes for which it is being processed, a description of any potential recipients of the data and any information as to the source of the data. In addition, the data subject has the right to prevent processing likely to cause damage and distress, the right to know the logic behind automated decision making and the right not to have significant decisions based solely on the results of automatic processing (for example psychometric testing for employment purposes and possibly admissions decisions based wholly on quantification of pre-entry examination results). There is also the specific right for the data subject to prevent processing for the purposes of direct marketing.

The transfer of personal data to countries outside the EU will be restricted unless those countries ensure an 'adequate level of protection for the rights and freedoms of data subjects'. This could be relevant when, for example, providing student transcripts to third parties overseas, the exchange of information for employment purposes, and the exchange of information on research grants and contracts. When determining adequacy, DPOs should consider the nature of the data, the country of origin and final destination, and the law, or any relevant codes of conduct, in force. Adequate protection of personal data may not be required where certain criteria are satisfied. These include where the data subject has consented to the transfer and where the transfer is necessary for the performance of a contract between the data subject and the controller. The Registrar intends to take a pragmatic approach to the issue of transferring personal data to third countries but will wish to see a high standard of adequacy whilst not unnecessarily disrupting international commercial data flows.

The new Act now covers information which is recorded as part of a 'relevant filing system' where the records are structured, either by reference to individuals or by reference to criteria relating to individuals, so that specific information relating to a particular individual is readily accessible. This definition will catch some types of manual data. Exactly what type of manual record is covered by this definition is still under consideration. The transitional arrangements will exempt manual records held in a 'relevant filing system' from compliance with much of the new law until 2007, but in the mean time DPOs should consider taking steps now to ensure that their information systems comply with the principles of good practice, regardless of whether the data in those systems are processed by manual or automated means. The government expects DPOs to take advantage of the transitional provisions and the application of exemptions. It is also suggested that DPOs should take a realistic attitude and not assume that the risk of error in records is so great that a complete review is needed rather than just correct the few occasional and inevitable errors when they are found.

Freedom of information ▪

The United Kingdom has lagged behind most major western democracies in not having a Freedom of Information Act. However, the government has promised to introduce such an Act which would give everyone a legal right to see information held by national, regional and local government, and some other organizations working on behalf of government. It is proposed that Freedom of Information would apply across the public sector at national, regional and local level so that this would cover not only government departments (for example Department for Education and Employment) and agencies (such as Employment Service) but also quangos such as the funding councils, schools, further education colleges and universities.

The intention is to make information available unless it would clearly cause harm, for example, to national security, the internal discussion of government policy, law enforcement, personal privacy, information which could unfairly damage a company's commercial standing, the safety of individuals, the public and the environment, and references, testimonials or other such matters given in confidence. Any decision whether to release or refuse information would need to satisfy certain basic tests (for example, is it lawful?) to ensure that it is consistent with the public interest. It remains HMG's intention to establish an Independent Commissioner.

It is intended that individuals have the right to ask for information and that organizations publish more information such as costs, targets, performance measures and complaints procedures for public services. This greater transparency could help institutions to gain more information and hence advantage when tendering for contracts (for example EU or commercial bodies) or when dealing with regulatory bodies so, for example, institutions could obtain more information on how teaching and research is assessed by funding bodies. Conversely, commercial companies could gain more information about the pricing of university contracts and members of the public may be able to ask for information on how decisions are reached when selecting students or staff. Until experience has been gained from the implementation of the Act it is not easy to see how universities can prepare for this. Good practice can be gleaned from the USA where such an Act is already in force. Many organizations in the USA have developed institutional good practice and much of this information is available across the Web. It is important not to overreact, but at the very least each institution will probably have to appoint a Freedom of Information coordinator and be ready to provide reasons for many of its decisions.

More significantly the knowledge that decision making will be open to scrutiny will encourage organizations to change the decision-making process. It will certainly be more difficult to hide from wider scrutiny the uncomfortable consequences of controversial decisions.

The impact of technology and the future role of administrators

The use of IT for data processing in areas such as admissions, student registration, student records and financial accounting has been commonplace in universities and colleges for many years. For many administrators the day-to-day impact of the IT revolution has come through the growing power of the desktop PC, the availability of user friendly software, and most significantly the use of intranets and the Internet. It is notoriously difficult to predict the development and impact of C&IT on the way we work, and this chapter will not fall into that trap, but instead will look at trends in how technology is changing the way administrators and their organizations work.

A pointer to this may be found in libraries where the 'access versus holdings' debate has been largely generated by a combination of the IT revolution and limited resources. Put at its simplest, are libraries places which own and store information by holding books and other materials against need, or are they locations (possibly real or virtual) where the 'customer' is helped to navigate the telecommunications infrastructure to gain access to the information they want at the time they want it? The issue is far more complex than this but changes to the role of administrators can be considered from a similar standpoint. The use of the Internet already means that documents from major official bodies can no longer be treated like state secrets, as these are often publicly available over the WWW long before they have reached the vice-chancellor's or principal's office. This easy access to information has increased the expectations of the internal customer so that administrators have had to make more and more internal and external management information available to all. The ability to work from home through Internet connections, the increasing availability of user friendly software, software that will allow the development of on-line management and administration and the control of work flow across departments and the institution, and the increasing use of integrated multimedia information systems are all part of a trend which is improving the availability of information, the ease by which information flows around and between organizations, and the ease with which information can be reformatted and manipulated. It is easy, for example, to envisage the development of on-line management committees where members can work together across the Internet (so they can be almost anywhere in the world) where they have access to previous decisions, are linked into easy-to-use formal management information systems, and have access to audio and video. The committee process will not be limited by time and space, and decisions can be rapidly communicated to the rest of the institution.

From these illustrations it can be seen how decision making can be put into the hands of 'the people', enabling a responsive, devolved management and administration, the delegation of information ownership, and the increasing use of more flexible working patterns. The role of the administrator as the guardian of the decision-making processes and the owner of the institutional information is fast disappearing. This is likely to shift the emphasis to working in partnership with the 'customers' adding value through provision of the highest quality information and data together with analysis and commentary providing the tools and infrastructure to access appropriate information in a timely way. Initially this may lead to many administrative roles requiring professional information specialists. We may then see that the creation of 'information service departments' in many universities will not only bring together libraries and academic computing services, but also include major parts of the administration.

Notes ■

1 R.N. Maddison (ed.) (1989) *Information Systems Development for Managers*. London: Paradigm Publishing with The Open University.

2 A. Pellow and T.D. Wilson (1993) The management information requirements of heads of university departments: a critical success factors approach, *Journal of Information Science*, 19: 425–37.

3 JISC Technology Applications Programme (JTAP) (1998) *Joint Information Systems Committee Technology Applications Reports*, which can be found at http://www.jtap.ac.uk/reports/index.htm

4 J. Meadows and T. Hopkins (1994) Surveys of information policies/strategies at British universities, in D. Revill (ed.) *SCONUL Working Papers on Information Strategies*.

5 Joint Information Systems Committee (1998) *Guidelines for Developing an Information Strategy*. Bristol: JISC.

6 Joint Information Systems Committee (1998) *Guidelines for Developing an Information Strategy – The Sequel*. Bristol: JISC.

7 D.K. Allen and T.D. Wilson (1996) Information strategies in UK higher education institutions, *International Journal of Information Management*, 16 (4): 239–51.

8 Ibid., p.242.

9 J. Fielden (1998) Collaboration in administrative computing: the issues, *ACU Bulletin of Current Documentation*, 134: 18–20.

10 D. Sangway (1988) Government approach to information management, *Aslib Proceedings*, 41(5): 179–89.

11 H.G. Morrison, S.P. Magennis and L.J. Carey (1995) Performance indicators and league tables: a call for standards, *Higher Education Quarterly*, 49(2): 128–45.

12 L. Wagner (1998) What is the point of university league tables? Unpublished paper to Committee of Vice Chancellors and Principals (CVCP) Conference on the Use and Abuse of University League Tables, London.

13 M. Yorke (1998) Don't believe the hype, *Guardian*, 23 June.

14 *US News and World Report* – College Rankings, http://www.usnews.com

6

MANAGING INFORMATION IN RESEARCH

David Squires

Global information seeking and communication sponsored by pervasive networks, combined with a range of ICT tools, will lead to radical changes in both the process and outcome of academic research – or at least this is fast becoming conventional wisdom. How realistic are such claims? From the researcher's perspective, are there significant changes in the way they seek information, communicate with colleagues, and report research? In terms of research infrastructure, are libraries required to conceive their roles in different ways with an emphasis on 'desktop' support and networked service provision? While there is evidence that radical changes are taking place, some of these changes are surprising. It is not simply a case that ICT will bring axiomatic improvements in efficiency and quality. Careful planning, based on a sensitive awareness of the needs of the user, will be essential if the potential of the use of ICT in a research context is to be realized.

The rationale for using ICT in research rest on four focal claims:

- Improvements in information access will make researchers better informed.
- New publication mechanisms will lead to improvements in the extent and quality of academic publications.
- The research culture will become more democratic, involving greater communication between researchers from diverse institutions at different stages in their careers.
- Research will be more efficient and cost-effective.

An emphasis on the process of research is evident in the first three of these: information access, publication and communication all stress process, with only the last emphasizing research outcomes. Given this focus on process, there is an implication that research into the use of ICT in research should employ methodologies which are capable of capturing the contextual richness and idiosyncratic nature of the research process. However, there is a strong tradition in library and information science research of employing quantitative research techniques in which contexts are well defined and users are conceived as stereotypes. This tradition is being challenged by the adoption of qualitative techniques which attempt to capture the rich diversity of information seeking and use from personal user perspectives. Fidel illustrates the possibilities of qualitative research in library and information science research.[1] Walster sums up the consequent changes in information access research as a move from sociological to psychological foundations; an emphasis on individuals rather than groups of users; quantitative, qualitative and combinations of quantitative and qualitative research adopted as part of user studies; and an emphasis on cognitive search strategies.[2]

In this chapter, the claims for the four focal rationales given above are discussed in light of the results of a British Library funded qualitative research study conducted between 1992 and 1996 at King's College London.[3-9] The study aimed to reflect the diversity and contextual richness of ICT use by researchers in the contrasting fields of education and high energy physics at King's College London. A novel qualitative methodology tuned to the specific context of using ICT in academic research was developed.[10,11] The methodology was rooted in the grounded approach advocated by Glaser and Strauss,[12] with changes in methodology being driven by feedback from ongoing data analysis. To capture contextual richness, a variety of data collection methods were used, including semi-structured interviews, diary completion, activity logs, biographical data, output measures such as number of publications and information access stories. The methodology stressed the synergistic analysis of these data to provide an holistic interpretation of the research process. The essence of this approach is summed up by Squires as 'borrowing from the ethnographic tradition'.[13]

Managing information access

The plethora of ICT systems now available, notably CD-ROM-based and networked systems, provides researchers with an enormous amount of both 'raw' and structured information. For example, the literary scholar has access to digitized versions of original texts, and the social scientist has access to huge demographic datasets. In addition there is a vast array of on-line bibliographic systems. For example, the education academics in the King's study had access to PsycLit and SocioFile CD-ROMs, and a range of networked systems including Education Resources Information Centre (ERIC), Bath Information Data Service (BIDS) and FirstClass. The theoretical physicists had access to a number of CD-ROMs and, most significantly, to the high energy physics, theoretical (HEPTH) pre-print bulletin board. A wide range of ICT information-handling tools are also available to both research communities: data analysis tools for quantitative raw data (for example, specialist applications such as DataDesk and general tools such as spreadsheets), data analysis tools for qualitative data (e.g. NUDIST) and bibliographic reference management software.

The research at King's has identified three salient issues concerned with the impact of ICT use on the process of information access:

* information overload
* synergies between different information sources
* the demise of traditional information sources.

Information overload

In some senses researchers are being offered too much information, or at least too much to know what to do with it. As well as the quantity of information increasing, the quality is becoming variable. This is illustrated by the emergence of the phenomenon of information overload, as illustrated in the following extract of the transcript of an interview with a high energy research physicist at King's:

Researcher: Well we sort of gave up because we had about three hundred papers and we didn't have the time and we were fed up doing it.

Interviewer: Did you find anything that was useful in that process?

Researcher: I guess the answer to that is no, so far, but maybe when this work gets a bit further – we'll really – we're aware that we should have read some of these papers and we haven't.

Interviewer: How do you decide which papers to read in this three hundred?

Researcher: Well you look at the title and you look at the abstract and you think whether it's of any interest to you.

Interviewer: Can you tell at that stage or have you really got to read it?
Researcher: Well that's the problem, you've really got to read it.

An even more extreme example is provided by another physicist, where information overload became 'information stress':

Researcher: Then I cancelled my subscriptions to [HEPTH]. Because otherwise it would fill up completely with anything... and I didn't do it again because I enjoyed not being overstuffed with all that information. I mean if you get onto this board and get 10 articles a day... and you just look it up for three days because you don't want to do it again and again...
Interviewer: It builds up.
Researcher: Yes, I'm not happy, actually, after a while, with this kind of system... it produces... an extreme stress.

These comments illustrate the negative effects that information overload can have. Given the central role that the use of the HEPTH bulletin board now plays in high energy physics research, the decision not to access the board amounts to a conscious disassociation from the research community. With the advent of information stress, researchers' use of information systems will decrease, leading to a reduction in their knowledge of up-to-date developments. In a more general sense, a feeling of not being able to cope with vast amounts of information may lead to a voluntary opting out of a research culture.

What can be done to help researchers cope with information overload? The development of criteria which researchers could use to assess the quality of unrefereed 'grey' literature would be very helpful. The need for such criteria is becoming ever more pressing as the amount of such material appearing on the Web keeps on increasing. Researchers can be taught good searching techniques and encouraged to develop searching skills tuned to their own needs. A researcher in education illustrates this point. He identifies a seminal article in a given field, and then broadens the scope of his information seeking by looking for citations of this article using a system such as BIDS. There is some evidence that routine information seeking can be automated, for example the regular mailing of the contents pages of journals to academics by email through systems such as Contents Direct. In the future it is possible that intelligent agents will perform regular routine searches using criteria specified by individual researchers.

Synergy between information sources

Researchers are faced with a bewildering array of information systems. These systems all have their particular strengths and weaknesses. It is very important that researchers understand the functionality of different systems so that they can use them in appropriate and efficient ways. The King's project found a number of instances of the 'screwdriver and chisel' approach, with systems being 'forced' to do things they were not really intended to do. However, other instances were identified where the functionality of systems was appreciated. This is particularly evident when systems are used in a synergistic fashion, with the features of each system complementing each other. This is illustrated by the use of a combination of an on-line library catalogue (Libertas), a CD-ROM-based bibliographic database (PsycLit) and traditional journals to complete a review of research literature in mathematics education:

> *Researcher:* . . . We said we'd use PsycLit and ZDM –
> *Interviewer:* ZDM?
> *Researcher:* ZDM is *Zentralblatt für Didaktic Mathematik* – a review – it's really a review of research in maths education. And just said the journals we'd look at, really, so it's a matter of finding out what we've got downstairs [in the departmental library], what's at the Institute [of Education Library, London]. So I've done quite a bit of work on that, going through – PsycLit has been very useful . . . I've used Libertas quite a lot in finding out where copies of things are.

The need for synergistic use of ICT systems has two major implications. First, there is a need for users to have accurate and robust mental models of how systems function, so that functionalities and strengths or weaknesses can be understood. Second, there is a need for user support to recognize the importance of synergistic use and to tailor user support to this end. Concrete illustrative examples are required which can be used by trainers.

The demise of traditional information sources

Barry highlights the demise of traditional information sources in her discussion of the use of ICT systems by the physicists at King's.[14] Pre-print bulletin boards, notably HEPTH, have become the *de facto* method of scholarly publication for this group. She highlights the radical effect that these boards have had when she states: 'There has been a direct negative relationship between the introduction of the bulletin boards and the demise of the use library. The academics in this team hardly use the library at all now.'[15] An exceptional visit may result from a need to consult an older paper, but as journals go on-line, even this need is diminishing.

Desktop access to bulletin boards and the like is obviously very convenient. However, there are some drawbacks. Libraries have an ethos which encourages browsing, a process which in itself can trigger new ideas and research directions. While it is possible to browse bulletin boards it does not have the same feeling of serendipity that scanning the pages of newly published journals has. There may be discipline-specific differences here. The physicists at King's seem relatively happy with bulletin boards as exclusive information sources, and to some extent they have replicated some of the less focused aspects of library visits with 'morning browses' of pre-print lists.[16] In contrast, the educationalists, working in a much more diverse and eclectic area, still value visits to the library.

The demise of traditional information sources is highlighted by the ongoing 'access versus holdings' debate. While notions such as the desktop library and the virtual library are no longer fanciful, the results from the King's study indicate that there are dangers in completely dismissing the role of the traditional library. The education researchers value visits to the library, enjoying the process of browsing through paper copies of journals. Indeed this browsing often acts as a spur for ideas, as the following extract from an interview with a researcher in education indicates:

Researcher: . . . On Cognition, I'm up to date, I mean recently I had to go back to see an article which was '89 and I made certain that I got right up to date on everything. Now I don't have any reason to go and look at Cognition again, because I've got all the articles. So I'm disciplined, the next time I will look at a different journal and get up to date on that.

Interviewer: Oh you mean the journal *Cognition*?

Researcher: Yes. Sorry, I'm not up to date on 'cognition', no. It's a question of browsing sensibly because otherwise you can spend a lot of time just looking through things, so each time I sort of bring myself up to date on one of the journals . . .

Interviewer: And did you find anything else while you were doing that?

Researcher: About four good articles, yes. Well I found, quite a
lot . . . If we do a new piece of research, I've got a lot
of evidence in articles there. I had a good look at
them, they're all very useful, so they're sort of sitting waiting for – there's a new piece of research I
want to do, on the force and motion thing, on the
theory of motion.

Perhaps 'surfing the Web' is not destined to completely replace the
library in the near future.

New publication mechanisms

The nature of academic publication is going through a period of
radical change, for example electronic journals, multimedia publication formats and electronic pre-print systems. There is a view that
these new forms of publication will lead to changes in academic
publishing. Three relevant issues have emerged from the King's study:

• increased peer involvement in publication
• enhanced multimedia presentations
• dynamic publication procedures.

Peer involvement

As pre-print bulletin boards and electronic journals become widespread, researchers themselves are becoming more active in the publication process. For example, some electronic journals now make
published peer reviews a feature. In the King's study Barry points to
the emergence of 'a new form of refereeing, in which all the readers,
including themselves, can review other papers, spot errors, suggest
improvements, offer additional references and so on'.[17] She cites
comments from the physicists at King's to support this assertion, for
example:

The paper comes out, it's put on the HEPTH list, and all the
others see it, of course. And then sometimes you get people
saying, 'Well this is very nice but what about such and such a
point?' When you put out the first version of the paper, when
we submitted it first to the HEPTH list, we didn't have that
reference and Tom and Clark pointed this out. Actually I know
him so I was happy to include that.[18]

Barry notes that researchers early in their careers, such as post-doctoral students, find this informal peer review particularly helpful. She also points out how peer review is moved forward in time, making it potentially more useful.

Multimedia presentation

Multimedia provides exciting opportunities for novel forms of research publications. Conventional journals are restricted to a mixture of text and illustrations, and the move to improve document delivery by making electronic versions of these journals is now well established. However, there are more novel developments, in which the nature of academic articles is changed, for example the inclusion of video and illustrative simulations in the body of the paper. While such forms of presentation are intrinsically attractive, there are clear implications for an increase in workload in preparing such papers.

Dynamic publication

As ICT use has expanded, information has become more dynamic. There is an implied need for researchers to keep up to date to ensure that their research has current value. In subjects like high energy physics, which are fast moving areas where new ideas and experimental results are appearing all the time, there is a sense of urgency associated with this dynamic nature. This is evidenced by the way that researchers at King's felt compelled to search the HEPTH database on a daily basis. In contrast, social science and humanities disciplines such as education do not feature the same rapid gestation of ideas and experimental results. Consequently the dynamic nature of new publication mechanisms is of less importance in these areas.

A democratic research culture

In many ways research can be an exclusive activity, with 'membership' of research communities being critical to keeping abreast of developments and ensuring that research findings are disseminated effectively. However, there is some evidence that the exclusive nature of research is being diminished by the advent of ICT. New technology is opening up possibilities for much broader participation in research, and in this sense participation is becoming more democratic. Dynamic and open publishing in electronic environments may ease the path to publication for researchers early in their careers.

The opportunity to communicate and collaborate with colleagues on a global basis may break down institutional barriers.

The HEPTH bulletin board provides a classic example of how dynamic publication can lead to a more democratic environment. Prior to the advent of HEPTH pre-prints in high energy physics were distributed by post to an elite groups of research institutions. The implication was obvious: to be involved in forefront research you needed to work at one of these elite institutions. Now the situation is very different, as with HEPTH existing on the Web it is accessible to all researchers in the field.

A finding from an Australian qualitative study illustrates how the communicative aspects of ICT can democratize research.[19] Dowling found that younger academics were using the information posted on personal Web home pages to establish working relationships with more experienced academics:

> It is of interest that several subjects, all younger academics, who would not at this stage have had any opportunities for face to face interaction with established researchers in their areas, whether in their own country or overseas, alluded to making regular and systematic searches of the home pages of other universities in search of details relating to staff working in the same or allied fields. Having located such people, several of the academics interviewed had gone on to make some form of contact electronically, all of them agreeing that this was less intimidating than the prospect of approaching unknown individuals either in person, on the telephone or by conventional mail.[20]

The move to a more democratic notion of involvement in research is extremely relevant in light of the relatively recent removal of the 'binary line'. There has been a rapid and significant increase in the number of academics who are expected to be research active. However, it is rather difficult to become a prolific and effective researcher overnight; academics can develop research experience and expertise only in a culture which nurtures the conditions for effective research. For most people, one of these conditions is frequent contact with colleagues, both as collaborators and mentors. Instances such as those cited by Dowling illustrate how the use of ICT can act as a catalyst for enabling such contacts.

Efficiency and cost-effectiveness

Qualitative research, such as that conducted at King's, is not geared towards the delivery of hard and fast evidence for efficiency gains and cost-effective practice. Questions such as 'Will providing access to information on demand be more efficient than maintaining holdings of publications?' are not appropriate to qualitative methodologies. Other approaches are more suited to looking at outcomes from an efficiency perspective, for example the approach adopted in a 1996 New Zealand study on *Valuing the economic cost and benefits of libraries* conducted by the management consultants Coopers & Lybrand.[21] In this study a profit-and-loss balance sheet was compiled on the basis of allocating value to benefits, revenue, turnover and cost. An analysis such as this has the advantage of an easily understandable representation, which can be very effective in broad brush strategic thinking. However, this sort of approach does not consider the process of information handling, a knowledge of which can point to proactive measures that are likely to improve efficiency and cost-effectiveness.

The findings of the King's study suggest some proactive measures geared towards effecting efficiency gains. There was some evidence that visits to the library by researchers were becoming more focused and less time consuming. The ability to do desktop catalogue enquiries can help the efficient use of inter-library loans services and prevent visits to external libraries only to find that the required publication is either on loan or unavailable for some other reason. Prior searching of on-line bibliographic services can make browsing visits to libraries much more focused. Wider dissemination of the notion of using ICT tools as a preparation for visits to the library could result in more efficient information-seeking behaviour.

Some of the negative findings of the study also suggest proactive measures. Clearly the issue of information overload needs to be tackled. Outcome measures which simply point to increased availability of information do not address the very real problems that researchers have in actually using this information effectively and efficiently. Much time can be wasted by sifting through masses of low grade and irrelevant material. The suggestions made earlier for developing quality criteria for information, highlighting innovative and effective search techniques, and automating searching are relevant here.

Conclusion

The results of the King's study are symptomatic of the messages emerging from qualitative work in library and information science. First, while there are many potential advantages associated with the use of ICT in a research context, there is also a down-side. Information overload, or its more extreme manifestation as information stress, needs to be countered by the development of criteria that differentiate good and poor quality information, researchers need to develop synergistic research techniques, and ICT design needs to keep pace with the demand of more automated information seeking. Rapidly dismembering traditional library facilities may not be the answer, as there is evidence, particularly in eclectic subject areas like education, that very constructive work takes place when traditional and ICT-based resources are used in tandem.

Second, new publication mechanisms are affecting the work patterns of researchers. Peer involvement in the refereeing process is becoming more informal and widespread. Multimedia affords challenging opportunities for the novel presentation of research findings. In some fields, particularly the sciences, the dynamic nature of publication is imposing a regular and frequent commitment to check bibliographic information sources.

Third, the research process is becoming more democratic. Institutional boundaries are becoming blurred as information is posted in a global context on the Web. Researchers from a diverse range of institutions now have the potential to collaborate and communicate, thus eroding the elitism that previously existed in some research areas. These developments are of particular significance to researchers who are early in their careers.

Finally, while the qualitative methodologies typified by the King's study do not yield definitive outcomes based evidence, they do provide a way of identifying techniques and approaches which may benefit the process of research, for example the use of ICT as a preparation for visits to the library.

In conclusion, the results of qualitative work suggest that the use of ICT is double edged. There are great possibilities for making information seeking much more comprehensive and richer, presenting results in motivating and informative ways, making research more democratic and pointing the way to more effective information seeking. However, there are dangers as well: information stress; the over-hasty disbandment of traditional libraries, and an erosion in the quality of information. The challenge is to overcome these dangers so that the four rationales presented at the start of this chapter can be realized.

Notes

1 R. Fidel (1993) Qualitative methods in information retrieval research, *Library and Information Science Research*, 15: 219–47.
2 D. Walster (1996) Technologies for information access in libraries, in D.H. Jonassen (ed.) *Handbook of Research for Educational Communications and Technology*. London: Macmillan Library Reference USA, pp.720–52.

3 D. Squires (1993) The use of information technology to support information access in research, in D.C. Johnson and B. Samways (eds) *Informatics
   and Changes in Learning*. Amsterdam: Elsevier Science, pp.183–5.
4 D. Squires, C.A. Barry and T. Funston (1994) *The Use of IT-Assisted Information Systems in Academic Research*, British Library Research and Innovation
   Department Report no. 6215. London: British Library.
5 C.A. Barry and D. Squires (1995) Why the move from traditional information – seeking to the electronic library is not straightforward for academic
   users: some surprising findings, *Online Information 95*. London: Meckler
   Press, pp.177–87.
6 C.A. Barry (1996) The digital library: the needs of our users, in *Proceedings
   of the International Summer School on the Digital Library*. Tilburg University,
   The Netherlands, 5 August 1996.
7 C.A. Barry (1997) Information-seeking in an advanced IT culture: a case
   study, in P. Vakkari, R. Savolainen and B. Dervin (eds) *Information Seeking
   in Context*. London: Taylor Graham, pp.337–56.
8 C.A. Barry (1997) Information skills for an electronic world: training
   doctoral research students, *Journal of Information Science*, 23(3): 225–38.
9 D. Squires (2000) The impact of new developments in information technology on postgraduate research and supervision, in J. Malone and B.
   Atweh (eds) *Aspects of Postgraduate Supervision and Research in Mathematics
   and Science Education*. Hillsdale, NJ: Lawrence Erlbaum.
10 C.A. Barry (1995) Critical issues in evaluating the impact of IT on information activity in academic research: developing a qualitative research solution, *Library and Information Science Research*, 17: 107–34.
11 C.A. Barry (1997) The research activity timeline: a qualitative tool for
   information research, *Library and Information Science Research*, 19(2): 153–
   79.
12 G.B. Glaser and A.L. Strauss (1967) *The Discovery of Grounded Theory:
   Strategies for Qualitative Research*. Chicago: Aldine.
13 D. Squires (1997) Exploring the use of interactive information systems in
   academic research: borrowing from the ethnographic tradition, *Education
   for Information*, 15(4): 323–30.
14 Barry, Information-seeking in an advanced IT culture, op. cit.
15 Ibid., p.352.
16 Ibid., p.249.
17 Ibid., p.348.
18 Ibid., p.248.
19 C. Dowling (1998) Academics on-line: changing academic practices in
   the age of the Internet, in G. Davies (ed.) *Teleteaching '98: Distance Learning, Training and Education, Proceedings of the XV IFIP World Congress,
   Vienna and Budapest*. Vienna: Austrian Computer Society, pp.292–301.
20 Ibid., pp.295–6.
21 New Zealand Library and Information Society (1996) *Valuing the Economic
   Cost and Benefits of Libraries*. Wellington: Coopers & Lybrand.

7

APPLYING TECHNOLOGY TO LEARNING: MAKING LINKS BETWEEN THEORY AND PRACTICE

Alan Staley

To cope with rapid change and the challenge of the information
and communication age, we must ensure that people can return to
learning throughout their lives. We cannot rely on a small elite, no
matter how highly educated or highly paid. Instead, we need the
creativity, enterprise and scholarship of all our people.

(David Blunkett, Secretary of State for
Education and Employment, 1998)[1]

The UK government's Green Paper, *The Learning Age*, outlined the
concept of lifelong learning – a vision that encourages adults to
enter and re-enter learning at every point in their lives, a vision that
sees learning take place in the workplace as well as outside of it, and
that opens up access for the many and not the few. The view that
learning finishes upon the completion of a degree and then work
takes its place, has never been a viable one. What is becoming
increasingly clear, however, is that the connections between academia
and the workplace need to be more explicit, and that teaching
methods need to adapt to enable this to happen. The simple information transfer model of education that sees the lecturer as a pump
attendant and the student as a container to be filled has no place in
this age. Instead, academics will need to come to terms with complex
dichotomies between the traditional academic environments and the
workplace. In particular, academics will need to help students connect
theory and practice, focus upon skills as well as knowledge, encourage

doing as well as understanding, and recognize tacit, experience-based knowledge alongside the more familiar academic knowledge.

Much has been made of the role of information and communication technologies in the Learning Age. Indeed, one could be forgiven for thinking that ICT is the panacea leading us to the Promised Land. Opportunities are clearly there for ICT to enable the visions of the Learning Age to come true, but there have been so many false dawns in the history of applying technology to learning that this optimism should be viewed with caution. This cautious optimism is reflected in the report of the Computers in Teaching Initiative (CTI) and Teaching and Learning Technology Support Network (TLTSN) review group:

> The majority of HEIs were found to be moving towards a teaching and learning strategy which explicitly incorporated CAL [computer assisted learning] and ICT. Perceived benefits of incorporating new technologies into teaching included greater access to and flexibility of study, and the extension of opportunities for distance, collaborative and networked learning . . . Many respondents felt the assumption that educational technology produced enhanced learning had yet to be proved . . . The vast majority did not expect the use of CAL or ICT to result in efficiency gains or economies.[2]

The benefits in terms of widening access, distance learning provision, and more flexible modes of study are clearly there to be exploited. However, many examples of using technology for learning have simply reinforced the dichotomy between traditional academic learning and the application of that learning in the workplace. Learning may now take place in front of the PC instead of in the lecture theatre, but this is still frequently divorced from the real world. The technology-led approach of 'here's some computerized subject content – now what do we do with it?' needs to be replaced by a curriculum-led approach that identifies an appropriate curriculum model that fits the Learning Age, and then identifies the appropriate use of technology for this model. This chapter is intended to show this, and identify good practice for making links between theory and practice.

A curriculum model for the Learning Age

> It is not enough just to do, and neither is it enough just to think. Nor is it enough simply to do and think.[3]

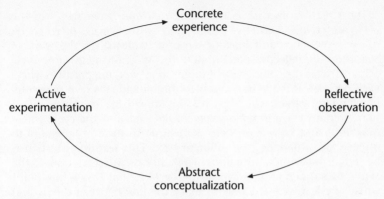

Figure 7.1 The Kolb Learning Cycle

The theoretical framework for this chapter is a well-established curriculum model which links theory and practice (Kolb).[4] This model is relevant in a range of educational contexts from continuing professional development to vocationally oriented undergraduate courses (see Figure 7.1).

The Kolb Learning Cycle

The crucial elements of this model are the links it makes between theory and practice or, in the words of Kolb, between concrete experience and abstract conceptualization. It is common for university courses to be described as either practical or theoretical. Similarly, it is often said that theories are taught at university but the real learning is what happens out in the workplace. However, it is not sufficient just to have an experience in order to learn. Equally it is not sufficient simply to learn new concepts. This learning must be tested out in new situations. The learner needs to make the link between theory and action by planning for that action, carrying it out, and then reflecting upon it, relating what happens back to the theory.

Experiential learning in the context of the model designed by Kolb involves a systematic, cyclical sequence of learning activities. The cycle may be entered by the learner at any point, but its stages must be followed in sequence. The interesting pedagogical issue is to develop appropriate learning and teaching strategies at each stage of the cycle. In other words, to provide structures which help learners to link theory and practice.

The *reflective observation* and *active experimentation* stages of the cycle are crucial. Reflective observation is the process of reflecting on an experience and making sense of it. Based on the work of Schon on the reflective practitioner,[5] this stage of the learning cycle acknowledges the complexity of professional working practices where each decision is made in relation to the individual's own repertoire of examples, values, commitments and knowledge. In reality, reflection overlaps the *abstract conceptualization* stage of the cycle where new ideas and knowledge help the learner to have insights and to understand situations in a different way. This learning must then be tested out in new situations. The author's interpretation of the active experimentation stage of the cycle is that this is the point where the learner plans how to make the link between theory and action. *Concrete experience* is therefore the practice: trying out the ideas in the workplace. The stages of the cycle are by no means clear cut. Considerable overlap can occur, as noted above. Work on Learning Styles indicates that just as there is seen to be a division between theory and practice in education,[6,7] so individuals may have particular preferences in their learning. Distinct styles of learning associated with the four stages of the experiential learning cycle have been identified, some learners being stronger at the practical aspects, others at the theoretical part of the cycle.

Application of technology to the curriculum model

The application of technology to this model assumes that students will need to break free from the computer in order to complete the cycle. It assumes that real experiences need to occur, and that lecturers will still have a very important role in the students' learning. The vision of virtual education is not represented here. I acknowledge that niche markets exist for distance learning and virtual education, but argue that for most further and higher education institutions, the way forward will be flexible provision that sees technology as a supplement, not a replacement. Each stage of the curriculum model is taken in turn, and appropriate use of technology considered (Figure 7.2).

Abstract conceptualization

Few subjects are totally content free or dependent purely upon learning processes. Indeed many subjects have a complex knowledge base, and academic staff spend considerable time in lectures expounding

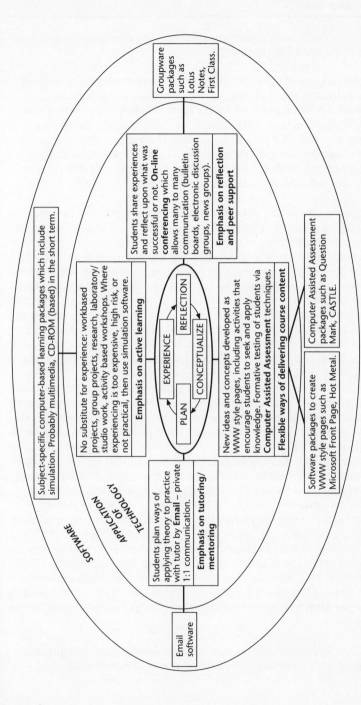

Figure 7.2 A model for applying learning technology to the experiential learning cycle

facts, theories, and concepts to students. The effectiveness of lectures has often been questioned:[8,9]

> I lecture myself (though seldom for more than fifteen minutes at a stretch and then seldom when written substitutes are available). I believe there are circumstances when a well structured, well paced, varied, lively lecture can be the most efficient teaching method. But I do believe there is far more lecturing going on than can reasonably be justified by the evidence concerning the efficiency of lectures, especially bearing in mind the nature of the educational goals we claim to be striving for.[10]

At least some of the educational goals we are striving for relate to equipping students with the skills that employers value. Harvey and Green indicate that specialist subject knowledge is often low down the list of employers' wants,[11] and that the ability to learn and adapt to a changing world together with communication skills are far more valuable. Sitting in a lecture theatre, passively absorbing information, does little to develop these skills. But does sitting in front of PC improve the situation? There are some benefits, for example the skills of searching for information and processing this independent from the lecturer, indicates more active learning, and develops self-reliance on behalf of the student. However, face-to-face communication skills are unlikely to be developed this way.

What seems a sensible way forward, however, is to replace some of the lectures by learning technologies, so that precious class contact time with students can be spent elsewhere in the cycle. In this way the role of lecturer will change from provider of information to that of nurturing development. Time spent developing skills and creating substitute experiences, if real ones cannot be found, will be far more appropriate in the Learning Age than the traditional methods of information transfer. There are no economies in this vision, simply a redeployment of academics' time to adapt to new demands.

Since the 1980s there has been a proliferation of computerized learning packages for use in higher education. In August 1992, the Universities Funding Council announced 43 projects that were to be funded under the Teaching and Learning Technology Projects (TLTP) initiative. This was extended in phase two of the programme and by 1996 over £70 million had been invested into developing materials that are largely free to HEIs. However, uptake of this material has been low:

> under-utilization of CAL and ICT remained a continuing, major problem for vitually all higher education institutions.[2]

There are many reasons to explain this underutilization, including lack of incentives for academic staff and lack of management commitment. The issue of change management needs to be clearly addressed, and academic staff development is crucial if the full potential of new technologies are to be harnessed. Incorporating learning technology within staff development programmes that are accredited by the Institute of Learning and Teaching (as recommended in the Dearing Report) would seem to be a sensible way forward.[12] Another reason that may partially explain underutilization is the ephemeral nature of the subject content in HEIs that limits the success of many courseware packages. The fact that subject content changes quickly, and that staff are always working in different contexts, can mean that such packages do not fit individual academics' requirements. Also many packages are trying to achieve all the learning via one package, including simulations to replace real experiences, rather than focusing upon part of the learning cycle or integrating with face-to-face teaching methods.

Academic staff need to be able to develop their own resources for the conceptualization stage of the cycle. The platform for these resources is without doubt the World Wide Web or the university or college intranet. This not only provides for the Martini view of education – any time, any place – but also provides for one point of update, eliminating the distribution costs of paper and CD-ROMS. Importantly, the increasingly easy-to-use authoring tools give individual academics the control and autonomy that they desire. However, the fact that academic staff can now create their own on-line learning resources has led in some instances to the creation of on-line lecture notes. This is unfortunate as it would appear that the history of resource-based learning has been forgotten. Rewriting the textbook was never an appropriate approach to developing resources, and many resource packs were destined to a life on the shelf because the processes with which to engage the students were not considered. Well-designed resource-based learning has objectives, learning activities that encourage deep learning (as described by Biggs)[13] and are written in a readable style. Such design principles are a good starting point for creating on-line resources, and would avoid, on the one hand, the automation of lecture notes, and on the other, expensively produced resources that add little to the students' learning, and which may be beyond the scope of most lecturers to create. Rowntree is useful for an account of how to develop open learning materials.[14]

The on-line resources that lecturers have created will be available for students to access in their independent learning time. That is not to suggest discovery learning, where students discover things for themselves in a haphazard way (such as by surfing the Net), but rather a focused pursuit of knowledge. Key to this pursuit of knowledge are the learning activities within the site. Some of these activities may be contained within the site that causes the students to conceptualize rather than merely passively absorbing information. Such activities might include defining features matrices, comparison matrices, one sentence summaries and many more. In the USA, such activities are referred to as Classroom Assessment. A compendium of these techniques is described in Angelo and Cross:[15]

• The one sentence summary challenges students to summarize large amounts of information about a topic in one sentence.
• The defining features matrix requires students to distinguish between closely related or seemingly similar items or concepts, using a simple grid structure having some features categorized and some blank for the students to provide their own.
• The comparison matrix asks students to write down as many similarities and dissimilarities as possible under a number of given headings.

Such activities will make the students think and take a deeper approach to learning. Activities can be designed into the site by way of an interactive form that the students submit to the tutor, or students can be asked to bring their work to the next seminar or workshop. An example of a relatively simple WWW page that encourages active learning as opposed to passive absorption is shown in Figure 7.3.

Elton has suggested that we should not always expect students to be intrinsically motivated by our subject,[16] and that students' intrinsic motivation will improve as they gain a sense of achievement or progress:

> contrary to what most teachers are likely to see as the best strategy, it is important to improve the examination preparation factor, which in turn leads to an increase in the achievement factor, long before an attempt is made to increase the subject interest factor, which should not be attempted until students have reached the low commitment stage.[17]

Two issues arise from this. First, we should not expect students to be intrinsically motivated by this on-line delivery for its own sake. Second, including elements of formative computer-assisted assessment (CAA) can be beneficial so that students can check their understanding of key issues, and receive feedback, before putting theory

Figure 7.3 A simple WWW page with learning objectives
and activities

into practice. Packages to create objective tests are widely available,
and such tests can now be included in the on-line resources. Such
testing can be very valuable for the first four stages of Bloom's
taxonomy:[18] knowledge, comprehension, application and analysis,
while synthesis and evaluation will be very difficult to test in this way.
Some simple computer-assisted assessment is shown in Figure 7.4.

The information provided by computer-assisted assessment is of
help to both student and lecturer. The students can clearly assess
their own progress, and receive helpful feedback of what to do to
improve their understanding of key concepts. The lecturer is able to
keep a degree of control, as the information provided would include
details of all students taking the assessment and the marks that they
have achieved. Valuable information will also be provided by showing the breakdown of marks by each question. This will help the
lecturer to identify topics that the students are misunderstanding, so

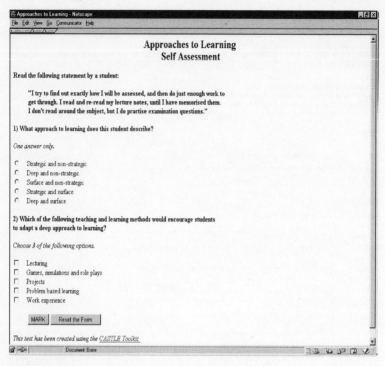

Figure 7.4 An example of Web-based computer-assisted assessment

that future seminars or workshops can focus on these, and that changes to the resources can be considered.

Concrete experience

So far, a controlled and very structured approach to creating on-line resources has been considered. This micro view of learning will be very important to some subjects because of the extensive knowledge base, and the volume of factual information that students must learn. However, conceptualization is only one phase of the learning cycle, and to represent a macro view of learning, the on-line resources should include activities that students must do for real in the concrete experience stage of the cycle. Real-world problems can be designed that are similar to those a professional would be faced with and that also necessitate students to cover all the important

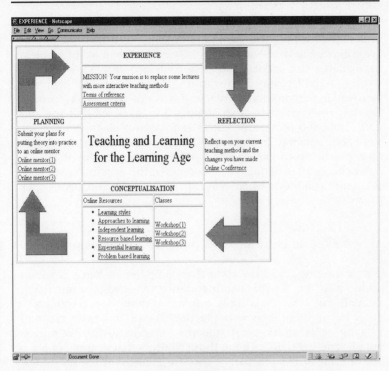

Figure 7.5   An example of a practical problem 'driving' the students' use of resources

parts of the syllabus. Students would be working on a need-to-know basis, consulting on-line resources as necessary, and learning what they need in order to tackle the problem. The large-scale nature of real-world problems should mean that students would not experience knowledge in artificially discrete packages. In this way, the students' learning is being driven by activities and problems, as described by Boud.[19] An example of this approach is shown in Figure 7.5: the problem drives the student's learning, the lower level resources shown here as hypertext links can then be more controlled as described earlier.

The approach suggested here, therefore, gives lecturers control at the micro level, and yet encourages independence at a macro level, as students solve problems in ways that are appropriate to themselves. Such an approach should enhance motivation, and yet still provide the necessary building blocks to enable the problems to be solved.

In the post-Dearing age of lifelong learning, it seems likely that work-based learning will grow, and links between theory and practice will need to be more explicit. Experiencing real-world problems is crucial to this model, and it is envisaged that where possible learning activities embedded within the Web site can be performed in a working environment. Where this is not possible (as in many full-time undergraduate programmes), it is suggested that academic staff create substitute experiences such as role-plays, mock courts and client briefings. In this way, class contact time is shifting from conceptualizing to experiencing. While I acknowledge that some experiences can be simulated by computer, this is considered to be a last resort, used only where real experiences are too dangerous, expensive or not practical.

Active experimentation and reflective observation

It is at these stages of the cycle that computer-mediated communication (CMC) is of particular importance. In active experimentation students can email their on-line tutor or mentor concerning their plans for putting theory into practice. The on-line tutor can individually guide and support students, offering advice, warning of pitfalls, and generally helping those students that cannot see a way forward. Email is particularly useful for students while they are in the workplace, for example part-time students, placement students and work experience students. Too often while at work, students consider the concepts that they have learnt at university to be theoretical and not relevant. The activity that students need to undertake in the concrete experience stage of the cycle may be seen as totally divorced from the theories in abstract conceptualization stage. Specifying in the activities that students need to email their lecturer with plans for linking theory and practice will make this connection much more explicit. Taking this planning one stage further, it is possible for learning contracts to be negotiated that focus upon learning objectives in the workplace, learning strategies to be adopted by the student, and evidence that the objectives have been met. A simple Web form could enable this contract to be created on-line.

Reflective observation is well suited to on-line conferencing, where groups of students can work cooperatively to reflect upon how the theories worked in practice, and how the different contexts in which students have been working have influenced this. On-line conferences enable students to interact with others and learn collaboratively. Students post messages to the conference for all of the group

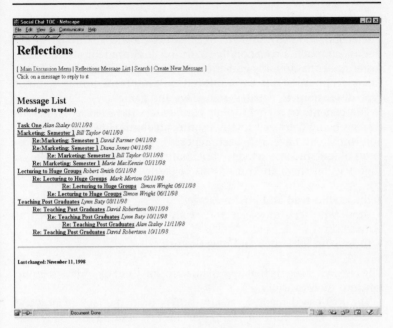

Figure 7.6 Using an on-line conference to reflect upon experience

members to see. This is therefore a public communication unlike the private email between student and tutor. An example of an on-line conference is shown in Figure 7.6.

The asynchronous nature of this form of communication is particularly suited to reflective observation as it gives students time to think and make a considered contribution. The fact that students can read and post messages to the conference at any time creates considerable flexibility. Such conferences therefore offer different benefits to video-conferencing for example, which because of the synchronous communication requires staff and students to participate at the same time. There may even be some benefits over face-to-face communication. In traditional face-to-face teaching environments, activist and pragmatist students often dominate discussions. The faceless nature of an on-line conference gives everyone the opportunity to contribute equally, and tempt the reflectors and theorists to contribute more. This democratizing effect has been well noted, particularly Dubrovsky et al.[20] and Steeples et al.,[21] in giving confidence to female participants and capitalizing upon women's team playing and cooperative skills.

The asynchronous conference emphasizes active participation and interaction, and helps students to construct knowledge through group discussion. Such a collaborative learning environment also helps to foster student autonomy and encourages a deep approach to learning. Many techniques can be employed on-line, from simple seminar type discussions to debates, role-plays and games.

The benefits of asynchronous conferences have led to numerous courses being delivered totally by this medium. However, considerable problems have also been reported, particularly the phenomenon of few students actively contributing to the discussions. Mason suggests that there are three kinds of participants in a conference:

- those who read and post messages
- those who read messages and rarely post (frequently labelled as 'lurkers')
- those who join once and never return.[22]

The research suggests that approximately one-third of a student group fall into each category.

The text-based medium clearly suffers from the lack of physical and social clues. Tone of voice, eye contact, gestures and body language that are so evident in face-to-face teaching are totally lost. A contribution to a conference is much more permanent than a comment said in class, and this can have a significant inhibiting effect. As with all forms of independent learning, motivation needs to be high; it is far easier to sit passively in a lecture and absorb information.

It would appear that on-line conferencing can enrich student learning, but that it is more likely to be successful if it is accompanied by face-to-face teaching and other technologies. In this mixed mode delivery there has to be a particular reason and place for conferencing. It appears that this technology lends itself best to the process of reflection upon experience. Students who have studied learning resources at a micro level, as discussed earlier, need to put theory into practice and experience real world problems at a macro level. Groups of students in the workplace or back at the campus can use the conference to reflect upon how theory related to practice, and hence complete the learning cycle. This type of discussion could be more meaningful than the more usual electronic seminar.

Summary

It can be seen that a number of different technologies have a place in the learning cycle, and each can add some value to the students' learning experience. Most importantly, face-to-face communication and traditional teaching methods should not be forgotten. The processes involved in teaching are just as important as subject content. Students' learning needs to be managed, and motivational factors considered carefully. Assessment has always been a driver of students' learning, but in the Learning Age this will become even more complex as learning in the workplace needs to be recognized and given credit.

The key question is how do we make best use of precious class contact time? Replacing some of the information transfer with learning technology could release time for more interactive teaching methods and perhaps allow more time for staff to create, and students to experience, real-world problems. Planning for, and reflecting upon, these experiences is crucial for effective learning to take place, and the technologies to enable this have been considered. However, providing these experiences for students is not always easy. Staff development will be vital to equip academic staff with new skills, and also to recognize their shifting role from information provider to facilitator. Such a change may appear threatening or at least uncomfortable to many staff, and how HEIs manage this change is of the essence.

Developments in technology are occurring at an ever-increasing pace. In terms of bridging the academia/workplace divide, the newly emerging technology of asynchronous multimedia conferencing (AMC) may be of help. Vivid representations of working practices captured as digitized video clips embedded within collaborative asynchronous discussions just might be the technology to explicitly link theory and practice.[23]

Notes ◼

1 Department for Education and Employment (1998) *The Learning Age: A Renaissance for a New Britain*. London: The Stationery Office.
2 M. Adkins (1998) Report of the CTI/TLTSN Review Group, *CTI News Online*, August. Available from http://www.cti.ac.uk/news/features/review.html
3 G. Gibbs (1985) *Learning by Doing: A Guide to Teaching and Learning Methods*. London: Further Education Unit.
4 D.A. Kolb (1984) *Experiential Learning: Experience as the Source of Learning and Development*. Englewood Cliffs, NJ: Prentice Hall.
5 D.A. Schon (1987) *Educating the Reflective Practitioner*. London: Jossey Bass.
6 D.A. Kolb, I.M. Rubin and J.M. McIntyre (1974) *Organisational Psychology: An Experiential Approach*. Englewood Cliffs, NJ: Prentice Hall.
7 P. Honey and A. Mumford (1986) *The Manual of Learning Styles*. Maidenhead: Peter Honey.
8 D. Bligh (1972) *What's the Use of Lectures?* Harmondsworth: Penguin.

9 G. Gibbs (1982) *Twenty Terrible Reasons for Lecturing*. Standing Conference on Educational Development. Birmingham: SCED.

10 Ibid., p.29.

11 L. Harvey and D. Green (1994) *Employer Satisfaction – Summary*. Birmingham: Quality in Higher Education Unit.

12 National Committee of Inquiry into Higher Education (1997) *Higher Education in the Learning Society* (Dearing Report). London: HMSO.

13 J.B. Biggs (1994) *Approaches to Learning: Nature and Measurement of the International Encyclopedia of Education, vol. 1*, 2nd edn. Oxford: Pergamon Press.

14 D. Rowntree (1990) *Teaching through Self Instruction*. London: Kogan Page.

15 T.A. Angelo and K.P. Cross (1993) *Classroom Assessment Techniques: A Handbook for College Teachers*, 2nd edn. San Francisco, CA: Jossey Bass.

16 L. Elton (1996) Strategies to enhance student learning: a conceptual analysis, *Studies in Higher Education*, 21: 57–68.

17 Ibid., p.65.

18 B.A. Bloom (1965) *Taxonomy of Educational Objectives, Handbook 1, Cognitive Domain*. New York: McKay.

19 D. Boud (1991) *The Challenge of Problem Based Learning*. London: Kogan Page.

20 V. Dubrovsky, S. Kiesler and B. Sethner (1991) The equalisation phenomenon: status effects in computer-mediated and face-to-face decision making groups, *Human Computer Interaction*, 6: 119–46.

21 C. Steeples, C. Unsworth, M. Bryson *et al.* (1996) Technological support for teaching and learning: computer-mediated communications in higher education (CMC in HE), *Computing and Education*, 26(1–3): 71–80.

22 R. Mason (1995) Scalability of on-line courses. Conference paper delivered at ALT-C (Association for Learning Technology-Conference), The Open University, Milton Keynes, 11–13 September.

23 P. Goodyear and C. Steeples (1998) Creating shareable representations of practice, *Association for Learning Technology Journal*, 6(3): 16–23.

8

INTELLECTUAL PROPERTY RIGHTS

Derek Law

Intellectual property rights (IPR) pose one of the least regarded, most complex and most dangerous areas of activity in education. Most institutions will have resolved how to deal with patents and their exploitation and probably with software written by staff. There is a tacit understanding to ignore issues concerned with publication of books and articles and this has implicitly but thoughtlessly been extended to the electronic arena, where something much closer to an anarchic frontier culture operates than the settled environment of the paper world. IPR is usually managed, if at all, by either the Research Office or its equivalent for IPR created within the institution and by quite junior administrators and/or librarians for IPR purchased or leased by the institution. Yet legally the registrar and the vice-chancellor or principal are at significant risk of personal prosecution because of such laxness.

Actions

The JISC, in one of its senior management briefing papers,[1] makes a number of sensible recommendations on intellectual property. The reasons behind these are explored further below, but the nine key points are worth highlighting as a useful checklist of recommendations and as a context to what follows. Few institutions will have made any real progress on implementing all of these recommendations.

1 All members of HEIs should be educated about copyright and what is acceptable.
2 All institutions should ensure that student regulations cover copyright infringement as a disciplinary offence.
3 All institutions should, similarly, update staff contracts.
4 All HEIs should ensure that copying of material is undertaken within the law.
5 All institutions should review what is made publicly available on the Web and implement controlled access to material which they are unwilling to see as in the public domain.
6 Institutions should ensure that systems are in place to seek copyright permission for material downloaded from the World Wide Web.
7 Institutions should review policy and contracts on all materials created by staff.
8 HEIs should educate staff in not giving away copyright in its entirety to publishers.
9 Institutions should have expeditious procedures for granting copyright clearance where this is sought from them.

Copyright, intellectual property and scholarship

The academic community is becoming more aware of the problems that are being caused by a failure to resolve this issue which has emerged as a problem. In 1999 an article explored how the system, which worked well for printed publications, is falling apart under the twin pressures of technology and copyright.[2] In the past, institutions allowed authors to sign away all copyright in all formats and in perpetuity in return for which the system assured that copies were distributed to libraries where they were permanently available and around which a system of indexing and referencing as well as inter-library loan has grown, which assured ready access to information. However, as material becomes electronic, the material is leased to institutions rather than owned by their libraries and is slowly accreting, at least in science, into the hands of large multinational companies with aggressive pricing and harsh intellectual property rights management. In a notorious case one publisher sued an American scholar who dared to suggest that their publications were bad value for money. It can cost thousands of pounds per year to subscribe to a major journal despite the fact that it is within the universities that the original research is largely conducted and the articles written. Major universities will spend over £1 million a year on journal subscriptions alone. In the UK and internationally, institutions have shied away from tackling the problem at its roots by asserting their own right to the intellectual property created by their staff. Only very slowly are major organizations such as the Committee of Vice-Chancellors and Principals (CVCP) beginning to consider whether some collective action would benefit the system as a whole. As Sutherland comments, 'Universities could lose proprietary control of the knowledge base which is their reason for being.'[3] Some aggressive responses are beginning to be heard. In the USA the Scholarly Publishing and Academic Resources Coalition (SPARC) was set up in 1997 by the Association of Research Libraries to underwrite the publishing of high quality electronic journals competing head-on with commercial products. All of the 114 member libraries have agreed to buy the titles. SPARC has now teamed up with the Royal Society of Chemistry to publish a journal *PhysChemComm* which will appear at a fraction of the price of its competitors.[4] Prophets of the end of scientific journals such as Ginsparg and Harnad have argued that savings of up to 80 per cent can be made if the scholarly community reclaims its own publishing.

This debate is being driven by the science, technology and medicine (STM) community, where the big money lies. Paradoxically exactly the opposite fear applies to other disciplines. Even in the largest university, STM rarely forms more than half the institution. Yet the electronic model that is emerging threatens the small almost cottage industry which publishes the research of these other disciplines. Small learned societies, often based in universities, will find it almost impossible to supply the level of technical competence or the global infrastructure which will allow them to disseminate journals internationally in the easy way that the postal system does. The Academy must begin to consider not how to fund the profits of publishers but how to create the global academic networks which will allow the sharing of knowledge which is the basis of academic life.

European legislation

Substantial legislation is under way at the European level although it is again librarians who are fighting the institutional corner. The proposed new EU directive on copyright is largely aimed at protecting the rights of commercial publishers and almost in passing poses huge threats to the scholarly community.[5] Unusually an advertisement was placed in *The Times* in February 1999 drawing attention to this threat. It brought together groups as varied as CVCP, Standing Conference of Principals (SCOP) and the Local Government Association to complain that 'The Directive is harming consumers at the expense of large multinational media conglomerates.'[6] Material created by that community is in danger of becoming inaccessible except at great cost.

Teaching materials

Librarians have complained about the situation regarding research results for some years with little effect. There is then a certain irony in the fact that it may be that the issue of teaching materials will be what forces institutions to act. The ownership of teaching materials ranging from course notes to examination questions has never really been considered by institutions, although a few newer universities do control this through staff contracts. Indeed few institutions will have any idea of how much it costs to set up a new course. In the past this has barely mattered while this was a purely internal matter. But recently something of a rush has begun to create Web-based courses, partly to allow students to learn when they like – asynchronous learning – and partly to ease the burden of course administration. The parallel growth of distance learning has also focused attention on the cost and quality of materials, with a general agreement that electronically delivered courses are very expensive to create. And yet many staff will assume that when they move from one institution to another 'their' course can go with them, despite the fact that the material was clearly prepared to further the work of the first institution. During 1998–9, geographers from several institutions set up a databank of examination questions to be shared by their community precisely because the creation of such questions is expensive and time consuming. It seems unlikely that many institutions will be happy to see their investment taken by staff to another institution, not least as the education market-place becomes more competitive. Most administrators will find it difficult to establish the present contractual position, far less enforce it, until there is some institutional commitment to address this issue, perhaps through a much more cost-conscious attempt to discover true costs. It should be noted in passing that some 'virtual' universities are paying academic staff to create courses for them and academics are willing to do this despite the fact that the virtual university may be in direct competition with their employer.

Academic staff often have a fairly cavalier attitude to copyright. Again this has not been critical when perhaps a cartoon has been shown on an overhead projector during a lecture. Similarly, a casual attitude to what might be libel or slander is accepted in a lecture, but takes a quite different face when placed on a network. Placing material on the Web, where the audience is massively larger, is a real threat to copyright and other issues such as data protection also come into play. Some institutions are beginning to appoint intellectual property rights managers. The University of Sunderland advertised such a post in *The Times Higher* to 'develop a strategy for recording and assessing all forms of research disclosure made by members of academic staff', while the University of Strathclyde has approved the appointment of a Digital Information Officer with the rather different role of managing the electronic assets of the university and its staff to ensure that they are protected, up to date and not exploited unfairly by third parties. The JISC-funded CATRIONA II project, also based at the University of Strathclyde, is preparing guidelines for institutions on managing such resources.[7] Incoming intellectual property also requires detailed management. A number of eLib projects, such as SCOPE,[8] have shown the increasing difficulty in obtaining timely and inexpensive permissions to use copyright material in support of courses and it seems inevitable that as institutions focus on courseware they will seek to encourage original content creation, rather than using supporting material from third parties.

Libel and slander

A little regarded but related area is that of libel and slander and yet these are activities which information strategies should address. Lawrence Godfrey, a UK physics lecturer, issued a writ against Philip Hallam-Baker, who works in a European research centre, complaining about material posted on a bulletin board. In June 1995 he accepted an undisclosed out of court settlement. Wessex Institute of Technology sued over newsgroup remarks that a conference it was arranging had low refereeing standards. Also in 1995, Peter Lilley, then a government minister, sued Leeds University over personal allegations made about him by a student on a bulletin board. The action was withdrawn when the offending material was removed. Under UK law it could be argued that the institution mounting the information was as liable as the individual. It should then be clear that institutions are responsible for *all* of the content and comment which is sent electronically from their networks. Institutions should review the contractual and regulatory environment in which they and their employees operate.

External users

Institutions are also at risk when signing licences for the use of electronic materials. These tended to be standard and are usually processed with little regard for the legal implications of the contract. The European Copyright Users Forum has a Web site which gives a useful checklist of things to watch for when signing contracts and is well worth further investigation.[9] Again this may seem remote but where institutions and their libraries or resource centres are used regularly by people from outwith the community there is a real danger that the licensee will pursue unauthorized use. The most obvious example is where NHS staff use HE or FE facilities.

Records management and archives

Most institutions will have more or less sophisticated records management systems for their paper materials. This percolates down to the department where departmental secretaries generally keep systems in order which allow the ready recovery of administrative information and correspondence. Yet most institutions will have a quite haphazard, indeed almost irresponsible, attitude to electronic documents. Readers will be familiar with the difficulty of remembering file names on their own PC. Many email systems automatically delete mail after a fixed period of time. There is little attempt to standardize document types – although some innovative work has been done on this at the University of Glasgow. Electronic archiving policies do not exist. This is no doubt partly because first generation exclusively electronic systems have only recently appeared and longer term issues of preservation and preservation standards have been able to be ignored and so have been. But such issues are much better addressed before data are lost and problems arise.

A variety of practices exist as far as paper archives are concerned. In same cases the archives sit managerially within the administration; in some cases there is a split between administrative and academic archives, which often sit within the library; in yet other cases all archives are managed by a professionally qualified archivist who can have variable reporting lines. One unremarked change has come about with the much wider involvement of institutions in training for health professionals. As a result many institutions have almost by accident become responsible for hospital and NHS records. These form part of the public record and as such are liable to public scrutiny by the Historical Manuscripts Commission. They will require that certain standards are met, particularly environmental standards such as BS5454 for the preservation of records. As yet no institution has suffered the ignominy of having records removed from its control, but that danger exists.

Nor should the proper management of administrative archives be seen as a necessary but tedious chore preserving material for some future historian. It can provide a small but increasing revenue stream. As more students attend institutions and as more institutions become involved in courses leading to qualifications associated with lifelong learning or continuous professional development they will have by definition a larger set of records regarding the performance of individual students. Certification that qualifications have been achieved or that grades were achieved is increasingly sought by both employers and former students. Fees can legitimately be charged for this service. Good well-managed archives will find a surprising number of both internal and external users.

Best practice

This chapter began by highlighting JISC's recommendations on copyright. It is useful to finish with the recommendations of the CATRIONA II Project. This Scottish Higher Education Funding Council funded project was led by Dennis Nicholson at the University of Strathclyde. It has attempted to identify the sorts of electronic content created by institutions and to look at standards associated with that and how universities should manage such IPR. It has produced a set of guidelines which are the only known work on this topic. There is then a certain irony that it is unclear whether the IPR in such guidelines is owned by the author, the university, the Funding Agency or is in the public domain! But institutions would do well to consider their implications.

CATRIONA II: intellectual property rights – draft guidelines

1 Aims

The aims of the guidelines set out in this document are to:

1.1 Provide a structure for the protection and exploitation of intellectual property created by university employees and to clarify the position with respect to ownership.
1.2 Preserve academic freedom while protecting intellectual property rights.

1.3 Encourage and stimulate innovative work by university employees by providing a framework for rewarding work of strategic or commercial value to the university. In respect of work of commercial value, the position set out provides for benefits that go beyond the statutory rights of university employees as set out in the following extract from the Patents Act 1977:

Employees' inventions: right to employees' inventions.

39 – (1) Notwithstanding anything in any rule of law, an invention made by an employee shall, as between him and his employer, be taken to belong to his employer for the purposes of this Act and all the other purposes if:

(a) it was made in the course of the normal duties of the employee or in the course of duties falling outside his normal duties, but specifically assigned to him, and the circumstances in either case were such that an invention might reasonably be expected to result from the carrying out his duties; or
(b) the invention was made in the course of the duties of the employee and, at the time of making the invention, because of the nature of his duties and the particular responsibilities arising from the nature of his duties he had a special obligation to further interests of the employer's undertaking.

(2) Any other invention made by an employee shall, as between him and his employer, be taken for those purposes to belong to the employee.

2 Definition of intellectual property

Intellectual property (IP), as referred to in these guidelines, includes, but is not necessarily limited to, multimedia packages, courseware, lecture notes, material subject to copyright, computer software, designs, video and similar material, animations, still images, audio items, research results and associated background material, and professional knowledge and skills. Essentially, it entails any intellectual output or associated skills that may be of strategic or commercial value to the university.

3 Intellectual property rights and strategic or commercial value

The university's position with regard to IPR in individual instances is determined by the extent to which the material in question is judged to be of strategic or commercial value to the university:

3.1 Material of relatively high strategic or commercial value.
Material in this category includes, but is not necessarily limited to:

- teaching materials of all kinds that are either currently in use or are intended for future use
- research and development materials of relatively high strategic or commercial value, including background materials such as research data that may be crucial to continuing research
- most software and multimedia material.

In respect of such material the university:

- specifically retains its rights as set down in the Patents Act 1977 (see 1.3 above)
- places on heads of department the responsibility for ensuring that access to the material is limited to members of the university only, except in instances where strategic or commercial agreements are in place or where funding body requirements specify the provision of wider access. This responsibility includes control in respect of access to electronic forms of material, including network access to such forms.

3.2 Material of relatively low strategic or commercial value.
Material in this category includes, but is not necessarily limited to:

- textbooks and chapters in textbooks and other similar works
- research and development materials of relatively low strategic or commercial value, including, in many cases, research papers and associated background materials.

In respect of such material the university:

- specifically waives its rights in respect of copyright, including electronic copyright (but see also Guidelines on Transference of Copyright below)
- retains the right to re-examine the strategic and commercial value of research material at any time and it charges heads of departments with the responsibility for reviewing the value of research material on an annual basis.

The decision to publish the material, whether in hard copy or in electronic form, rests with the individual member of staff concerned, but is subject both to any legal restrictions resulting from earlier transference of copyright and, in respect of electronic publication, to the university guidelines on electronic publication set out in Appendix 2 below. Responsibility for ensuring that both legal restrictions and university guidelines are adhered to, particularly in respect of networked electronic publication, rests with heads of department.

4 Determining and monitoring strategic or commercial value

Responsibility for determining and monitoring the strategic or commercial value of intellectual property created by university staff in the course of their duties rests with heads of department.

University procedures in respect of this process are set out in Appendix 3 below. Individual members of staff are responsible for consulting the department head prior to publishing or otherwise communicating material that may be of strategic or commercial value.

5 Rewards for work of strategic or commercial value

The university aims to encourage and stimulate innovative and other useful work by university employees by rewarding work of significant strategic or commercial value according to the guidelines set out below in Appendix 3.

Appendix 1: copyright assignment or transfer – awareness of the implications

1 All members of university staff should be aware of the implications of agreeing to transfer ownership of copyright to publishers and of the advantages to themselves and the university of considering alternatives, such as insisting on the retention of certain rights or of only granting a limited licence to the publisher for the use of the copyright in certain circumstances. To this end, they are advised to attend the Intellectual Property Rights Course offered by the Centre for Academic Practice in conjunction with the Research and Consultancy Office and the university copyright officer.

2 Before agreeing to transfer ownership of copyright to publishers, staff should consider, in conjunction with their head of department, and the Research and Consultancy Office, the likely commercial and strategic value of the work concerned. Where a work is judged to be of commercial or strategic value, negotiations with regard to rights transference must be concluded in conjunction with the Research and Consultancy Office.

3 It is common practice for publishers to request or require authors to assign their entire copyright to the publisher and the university recognizes that authors may often find it necessary to agree to

this. Authors should be aware however, that this practice can often put themselves and the university in the position of buying back subsequent uses of their own work and should consider the advantages of retaining certain rights. In particular, authors are encouraged to negotiate the retention of rights for on-site use in hard copy and electronic form, for on-site teaching packs, for on-site delivery of articles in hard-copy or electronic form, the extension of these rights to the university's strategic partners, and for inter-library borrowing and lending.

4 In addition, where publication in the one form (for example hard-copy) is the intention, rights to publish in other forms (such as electronic) should, if possible, be retained. The university manages a service which aims to exploit the commercial, strategic and promotional value of the electronic forms of all works created by university staff by providing (as appropriate) controlled or free access to other universities. Where possible, the needs of this service should be considered when transference of rights are being considered.

5 The university maintains a database of information related to the transfer of copyright on works created by its staff. Full details of all agreements or copyright transfers made by staff must be recorded in this database.

Appendix 2: guidelines on electronic publication

1 The aims of these regulations/guidelines are to encourage the electronic publication of high quality research and teaching resources, and the process of academic communication, while at the same time seeking to ensure that the university and its staff:

- do not infringe copyright laws and regulations
- are protected against the infringement of their own intellectual property rights by others.

2 Members of university staff must make themselves aware of the university guidelines on the transfer of copyright and should aim to retain the rights to electronic publication of material whenever possible. Where such rights are transferred to another party, the transfer should be logged in the database of such transfers maintained by the university. Members of the university staff must not publish materially electronically where they have transferred this right to another party.

3 Members of university staff must make themselves aware of university procedures for determining and monitoring strategic or commercial value of intellectual property created by university

staff and should ensure that access to electronic material regarded as being of high strategic or commercial value is only available to individuals or groups with appropriate security level accreditation on the university intranet. This is particularly important where the groups or individuals concerned are not members of the university.

4 Members of university staff intending to publish material electronically are advised to consult the university's information Office who will advise on:

- pre-publication on the Web
- subsequent hard-copy publication
- metadata standards required for inclusion in university e-resource service
- quality and design standard for inclusion in university e-resource service
- alternatives to direct mirroring of hard-copy publications or the Web and vice versa.

They are also advised to consult the Research and Consultancy Office regarding pre-planning to enhance the strategic or commercial value.

5 Heads of department are responsible for ensuring that:

- members of staff in their departments are aware of these university regulations
- members of staff do not infringe copyright through electronic publication of material for which publication rights have been transferred to another party.

Appendix 3: procedures for determining and monitoring strategic or commercial value, for protecting such work and for rewarding associated staff

1 The aims of these guidelines are both to allow the university to identify, protect and exploit intellectual property that is of high commercial or strategic value, created by members of staff in the course of their duties, and to put in place procedures to reward staff concerned through:

- offering staff reasonable remuneration beyond their statutory rights where commercial exploitation is involved
- offering grade-related and/or increment-related rewards for work of high strategic value.

A key concern in carrying out this aim will be to protect both academic freedom and the process of academic communication.

2 Members of staff embarking on new research or development work should seek advice on assessing its potential commercial or strategic value from the Research and Consultancy Office, who will also advise on pre-planning to enhance potential strategic or commercial value, register work of potential strategic or commercial value in the research and innovation (R&I) database, and advise on publication decisions, public relations (PR) protection, and exploitation.

3 The Research and Consultancy Office shall be responsible for advising staff on the matters outlined in 2 above in the best interests of both the university and the member(s) of staff involved, while at the same time seeking to protect both academic freedom and the process of academic communication.

4 Heads of department shall be responsible for:

- advising members of staff in their departments about these guidelines
- ensuring that members of staff in their departments are given due credit during annual review procedures for having created works of high strategic value to the university of the department
- ensuring that members of staff embarking on research and development initiatives seek the advice of Research and Consultancy as regards potential strategic or commercial opportunities at the earliest possible opportunity
- ensuring that intellectual property assessed as being of low commercial or strategic value is reassessed on an annual basis and a decision taken within the department as to whether a reassessment by Research and Consultancy is required
- protecting intellectual property of high strategic or commercial value by restricting access to associated local publication while at the same time protecting academic freedom and the process of academic communication.

Notes

1 JISC (1998) *Copyright*, JISC senior management briefing paper no. 5. Nottingham: JISC Assist.
2 J. Sutherland (1999) Who owns John Sutherland?, *London Review of Books*, 7(January): 3–6.
3 Ibid., p.4.
4 D. Butler (1999) The writing is on the web for science journals in print. *Nature*, 397: 195–200.
5 See for example a 1998 report in the *Library Association Record*, 100: 393.

6 *The Times*, 8 February 1999, p.8.
7 http://wp269.lib.strath.ac.uk:5050/Cat2/index.html
8 http://www.stir.ac.uk/infoserv/scope/
9 http://www.kaapeli.fi/~eblida/docs

9

TOWARDS THE ELECTRONIC LIBRARY

William Foster

The push towards the electronic library which is currently taking place has come about because of a number of factors, most of them to do with the networking of computers both individual and institutional.

> That this electronic revolution in libraries has occurred, of course, is due to developments over which the library profession has had little or no control, most obviously the growth of electronic publishing and of networks that facilitate scholarly communication.[1]

With extensive campuses, large student numbers and widespread use of technology, many US educational institutions have been exploiting aspects of the electronic library since the early 1990s. More recently other countries, including the European Union, have initiated extensive research programmes with the implications of the development of the electronic library as the central focus. In the UK for example, the Electronic Libraries (eLib) programme, a direct response to the 1993 Libraries Review commissioned by the UK Higher Education Funding Councils, has an overall aim 'to engage the Higher Education community in developing and shaping the implementation of the electronic library'.[2] The review was critical of UK higher educational libraries' failure to embrace technology for the development of networked electronic information services in order to alleviate some of the problems brought about by declining book funds, and went on to suggest that:

there needs to be a sea-change in the way institutions plan and provide for the information needs of those working within them. The traditional view of the library as the single repository of information needed for teaching, learning and research is no longer adequate.[3]

More recent UK government reports (discussed in Chapters 2 and 3) have highlighted the need for academic institutions at all levels to utilize technology more fully, and to integrate it into their programmes of study to improve teaching and learning for an ever-growing student body of lifelong learners. Such developments are likely to be a major driving force in the speed with which the electronic library is implemented, but how quickly this happens in different institutions will depend upon the willingness of senior management to put in place the necessary technological infrastructure.[4]

The electronic library

The electronic library can be described as the utilization of one or more networks to deliver a broad range of electronic information to the user's desktop.

While physical library collections are bounded by space, being located in a set of actual buildings and usually based in one (possibly distributed) organisation, the electronic library is potentially freed from these constraints. So electronic or digital libraries could be organised in various different ways, including an institutional basis, but also possibly regional, or subject-based.[5]

The move away from providing and maintaining a physical print based collection to providing a networked library of digital resources will clearly bring with it a culture shift for both librarians and library users.[6] The electronic library will bring a significant number of differences with which librarians, academics, researchers and students will need to contend. Librarians will increasingly need to provide their traditional services and any new services in some electronic form rather than expect face-to-face contact with their customers. Resource items will become non-returnable because multiple copies of individual items can easily be created on demand. As academics become both more willing and more accustomed to using electronic information, they are likely to become increasingly dependent upon technology for information access. Information providers can supply their information directly to the end-user, thus bypassing the library, and raising the question of how much the shape of the electronic library should be or will be end-user driven. The move to an electronic information environment will radically alter the way that a library operates and interacts with its traditional customers and it is no surprise that despite the general trend and the growing impetus from outside, some libraries have been slow to move in the direction of the electronic library.[7] Even large research libraries with vision have felt bound to move with caution. The third and final phase of the eLib programme has introduced the concept of 'hybrid libraries' which offer a way ahead for those institutions with large historic paper-based collections. These are discussed more fully below (p.139).[8] Librarians will need to consider their own future role as intermediaries, and evaluate how much resource selection, service direction and user guidance they will need to continue to provide within their institution, bearing in mind that many academics may be very conservative in their use of information resources. Furthermore some subject areas which are not print based, such as fine art, music and archaeology, will require considerable effort in converting their resources into electronic form. Nevertheless many of those in educational institutions now recognize that:

> the pace of development in digital techniques has seen a continued decline in the cost of hardware and software along with an increase in performance system components. There have been improvements in the areas of materials acquisition, image and text management, viewing and distribution systems, and printing and charging mechanisms

all of which suggest that the time is ripe for libraries to move towards substantial electronic resource provision.[9] This chapter will discuss some of the issues surrounding the transition to the electronic library.

Information services in the electronic library

The electronic library will form a crucial part of an institution's information services provision. This will increasingly have a much wider remit than that of the traditional library, encompassing both academic and administrative information designed to support all activities that the institution undertakes.[10] The UK's HEFCs Libraries Review suggested that university libraries should be more involved in helping shape university information policy,[11] for as Watson says, 'information services contribute to the institutional development through the activities of information management, information technology and learning support.'[12] Irrespective of the specific information direction taken by an individual organization, the information service manager responsible for the electronic library will need to consider a number of issues relating to the provision, control and flow of information in an electronic environment. These issues will be a mixture of managerial and technical, and although a number of them will already have been encountered in the traditional print-based library, the move to an electronic environment will add an extra and more complex dimension. Ideally the library, in conjunction with the institution will develop an electronic information policy framework (see for example Graves)[13] which will address issues such as:

- resource creation
- collection development
- archiving and preservation
- access provision
- document delivery
- publishers, publishing and publications
- training and awareness
- individual user needs
- performance measurement.

These could be grouped more usefully for the new electronic environment, as suggested by Brophy and Wynne:[14]

- resource discovery
- resource delivery
- resource utilization
- infrastructure provision
- resource management.

McLean has suggested that there is a need to map both the technological and information infrastructures necessary to support the desired outcomes of the electronic library:

> The challenge is to integrate diverse proprietary systems into the Internet environment in a way which allows the customer to share the illusion of seamless access for both resource discovery and the delivery of information in both electronic and print form.[15]

For the information service manager the biggest problem is perhaps the lack of a model which can be used to establish a working framework linking the resources, services and technical infrastructure required to deliver an institution-wide information system. Mel Collier, former head of the Division of Learning at De Montfort University, one of the pioneering converged services in the UK, has commented:

> the digital library work had no base of prior experience else-where. The examples of the management of change under the technological imperatives we were subjected to were few. Early library automation was to do with changing processes and looking for technical efficiency. The electronic library is changing the way the library works. We are potentially changing the content of the library, the interaction between the users, the material and the staff.[16]

Electronic libraries will need to provide a range of services for internally generated and externally acquired academic and scholarly information, and may be involved in the delivery of administrative information as well. However, the primary aim of the electronic library will be to support the institution's teaching and learning. The quality of the information content of the electronic library will be crucial to its success, as will its promotion to, and support of, different client groups.[17] Libraries will have an opportunity to increase their present role in providing help to users in resource selection through value added services ranging from the provision of subject gateways to personalized resource packs for individual academics and students. The exact nature of the information service provided will clearly vary between different institutions as it has always done in the traditional library environment. Sloan provides a wide range of opinion from different US librarians in his paper on service perspectives for the digital library where scenarios range from the complete redundancy of librarians to the all-powerful librarian controlling all access.[18] For most libraries the final scenario will surely lie somewhere in between with challenging new roles for librarians, but the problem of where to draw the necessary lines between information support, learner support and technical support is likely to remain, as discussed by Bartle et al.[19] and by Rapple.[20] The eLib IMPEL2 project has collected data from a number of UK educational institutions 'in order to identify the key issues surrounding the effective management of information services on the electronic campus'.[21] In the short term all that most libraries will be able to do is to determine the current needs of their users and to provide a variety of pilot and experimental services, recognizing that the electronic library will form part of a much wider electronic teaching and learning environment. One of the early pioneers of the electronic library, Tilburg University in the Netherlands, suggested that the central elements of a successful electronic library are 'an infrastructure based on a campus-wide accepted computer architecture, integration of services and personally controlled information management'. After eighteen months' operation they recognized that in the short term

> the future will not simply be the 'the electronic library'. The full electronic library without staff and real books will do a poor job in the next decade and will not be able to meet all user needs in a research environment. On the other hand, a library that does not give access to electronic information will disappear and will, at best, become a museum.[22]

Resource creation

Libraries have been providing access to electronic resources for a number of years, but 'in a relatively short period of time, electronic resources have expanded from a few dozen computerized bibliographic databases to include the overwhelming information available on the Internet'.[23] In the short term the resources to be found in the electronic library are likely to mirror those created in the traditional print environment. However, most academics are now using office software to produce scholarly papers and to create teaching materials, and it is increasingly likely that many of these resources will be placed in the institutional (if not public) domain without recourse to the traditional publishing process. The rapid growth of institutional internets, or intranets, is encouraging academic staff to make teaching and learning materials more widely available. CATRIONA II was an eLib-funded project examining approaches to the creation and management of electronic research and teaching resources at Scottish universities. This was a wide-ranging project exploring a number of key questions relevant to academics and their use of electronic resources. The questions asked were:

- To what extent are academics creating acceptable electronic research material?
- To what extent are they creating electronic teaching material of value beyond the local institution?
- Is the material in deliverable and usable form and is it accessible? Is it important to academics that it should be?
- Will universities create and manage services to deliver such resources to the desktop either within or beyond the local institution?

- What are the institutional, as well as operational, requirements of such services, and what if anything, is the role of the library in terms of policy, strategy, organizational and infrastructure and related matters?

Alongside these key issues the research also investigated:

- the balance of research and teaching responsibilities
- use of different desktop computing platforms
- availability of network facilities within institutions
- transference of copyright ownership
- factors which were likely to encourage electronic resource creation among academics.

The survey results showed on the one hand that a significant amount of research and teaching material exists (90 per cent reported they have such material), but that it is not generally available (69 per cent) and that even accessible material may require further electronic conversion or the use of specialized software products for access and viewing, and may be difficult to find. On the other hand 85 per cent of academics regard desktop access to resources created at other institutions as either important, very important or essential.[24]

Local resources

A particular problem faced by institutions is the accumulation of a range of disparate electronic resources acquired or licensed by individual departments or schools of study. Academics are creating a range of materials for teaching and learning in a wide variety of formats and there is often a complete lack of standardization within a department – far less an institution. The formats used to create teaching and learning materials include:

- standard office software files (word processing, spreadsheet, database, presentation)
- Web pages (using different versions of html)
- digitized non-electronic text and image resources (converted to PDF, GIF, JPG and similar image display formats).

Many of these resources are likely to be made available across the institutions intranet in a fairly haphazard fashion and it will be important to impose standards of page design and Web site structure in order to ensure that the intranet as a whole is efficiently constructed and usable by students and staff alike.

Academic departments are now frequently taking out their own subscriptions to information providers thereby bypassing the usual library acquisition service. It may be that in some cases departmental licences are cheaper because of existing professional or other memberships. But often this will not be the case, and faculty or subject librarians may sometimes have to act as broker on behalf of those department who are keen to acquire resources independently, in order to ensure the best value for the institution as a whole.

Individual academics using the Internet are signing up for a wide variety of electronic services including mailing lists, newspapers, current awareness services and personalized news bulletins. Many of these will be free, or free on a trial basis, but other services may have a cost implication such as transatlantic access charges, as introduced by the JISC in 1998. Some might duplicate what has already been subscribed to centrally and take up valuable bandwidth on the local network. Other services might be substandard compared to what is already on offer through the electronic library service. Librarians will need to work tactfully with academics to ensure that on the one hand they do not dampen local enthusiasms and continue to provide encouragement in electronic resource use and Web page construction, but on the other hand point out the benefits of using centralized resources and subject gateways wherever possible.

Collection development

For those involved in developing electronic collections there are a number of issues to consider such as subscription arrangements, resource selection, access and delivery mechanisms, and maintenance procedures. Many educational institutions will have had to tackle these issues in respect of CD-ROM collection policies. However, a more holistic approach may be required where a library is planning to switch exclusively to electronic resource provision. In the long term it is likely that scholarly and pedagogic resources as we know them will evolve to take account of the new electronic environment. Ghikas said in 1989 that:

> the twenty-first century collection will, I believe, be an accumulation of information bearing objects – printed, aural, graphic, digital – housed within the physical library, and also indices, abstracts and catalogs through which, using electronic channels the library user has access to pre-identified resources held by

other libraries and information providers. The twenty-first century 'collection' thus combines the actual and 'virtual' collection.[25]

Libraries not only will have to decide how much to hold and manage in electronic form, and how much in traditional form, but also will have to decide how much to access from available regional or national digital collections. This raises two important questions: how large a central library, if any, might be required in the electronic library, and what will be the likely nature of externally available collections? Libraries will certainly not be expected to carry the full burden of electronic resource provision themselves. The British Library,[26,27] for example, has a number of priorities for its digital library including:

- the establishment of an infrastructure capable of supporting the extension of UK legal deposit legislation to electronic materials
- the expansion of British Library document supply services built on article alerting and improved requesting and delivery from a digital store
- the expansion of patent service
- improved access to the Library's historical collections through services for researchers, schools and the general public
- integration of these developments into the mainstream of British Library collections and services.

The UK higher educational community has been fortunate in having a number of electronic resource collections available for use since the establishment of its network infrastructure JANET in the early 1980s. Funded by the UK HEFCs through JISC, these collections include a mixture of published and non-published sources distributed at various centres around the UK. During 1995/6 JISC has developed a collections policy for what it calls the Distributed National Electronic Resource.[28] The continued provision of a particular resource within a nationally maintained collection will clearly depend upon its use and cost-effectiveness, and criteria will need to be developed for review and reassessment. Clearly such criteria could be applied to institutional and even departmental resource provision as well. JISC have suggested that these may include:

- the fall of usage levels below an acceptable norm
- the availability of content elsewhere to a higher degree of quality or at a considerably lower cost
- content that has been superseded or is no longer sufficiently accurate to justify maintenance in active form
- expiry of a limited licence and withdrawal/return of a dataset to the supplier

- cost to sustain access to the dataset outweighs the value/benefit received
- poor quality service, or inaccessibility of content due to poor quality indexing, imaging or other characteristics internal to the dataset
- preservation, conservation and archiving migration, and storage needs of datasets that are deemed to have an enduring value to the nation.

Archiving and preservation

Because digital information is forming a growing part of our cultural and intellectual heritage, there is an urgent and growing need to archive and preserve all manner of information which may be useful to future scholars.[29] Griffin in his review of the US Digital Libraries Initiative has remarked that 'The quantity of online digital information is increasing ten-fold each year in a relatively uncontrolled, open environment.'[30] Not only must this information be preserved, but also the means to access and view the information must be preserved alongside it. This means that a range of appropriate hardware platforms, systems software and viewing browsers will need to be retained, and maintained, for consulting historical material long after they have been superseded by more technically advanced versions for current use. This may have considerable implications for libraries as they migrate from one electronic library system to another over time. A number of US information managers and computer scientists such as Gladney[31] and Lyman and Kahle[32] have examined some of the technical problems surrounding the safeguarding of digital library content. Scientific and technical subject areas have been building and using digital collections for a number of years, but as more social scientists and humanities academics begin to do likewise there will be a growing proportion of qualitative and multimedia information to add to the existing collections of digital quantitative information. The Arts and Humanities Data Service, a JISC service funded from 1995/6, has recognized that there are many problems in this particular subject area to be addressed, and only with the widest possible consultation will long-term standards and cooperative agreements be reached.[33] The funding councils have also invested some £50 million in electronic libraries, which has been provided for the digitization, cataloguing and preservation of humanities collections in the little known and unfortunately titled Non-Formula Funding for Collections in the Humanities initiative (NFF for short). This programme ran from 1994 to 1999.[34] It has been succeeded by the Research Support Libraries programme[35] which is distributing a further £30 million to support the creation of better catalogues of library resources, some digitization and general sharing of resources. This programme follows from the work of the Anderson Report,[36] which called for greater investment in resource sharing through making information about library collections available electronically. It was and is particularly concerned to see cross-sectoral resource sharing.

Access provision

Access to electronic resources will need to be considered from a number of different perspectives – user, subject discipline, information providers and the available technical infrastructure. Users will want to access the available information from different locations, such as the office, library, laboratory or home, possibly using different hardware and software platforms. Should the interface to the resources of the electronic library be developed to a lowest common denominator, or will it be acceptable to expect every user to download and/or install any additional software products necessary to view the resources? Alternatively, should different front ends be provided to different user groups or for different resource types? At the present time many institutions are limiting their user interface to what a standard Web page can offer, with the result that many journals, documents and multimedia resources created using non-Web formats by external information providers, cannot be viewed without additional software. This is a problem likely to continue until document creation and handling standards are commonly agreed, particularly for more complex material such as maps and images. Digimap offers a good example of a project exploring issues surrounding the provision of access to non-book material which is expensive to produce in print form and which is subject to continuous update. Digimap's aim is to examine the difficulties facing HE map libraries in providing electronic access to Ordnance Survey digital map data such as the choice of the ideal viewer/browser and the technical skills required to use it, and users' requirement to download the data into desktop Geographic Information Systems (GIS) software.[37]

Many research projects are tackling the problems of resource access in the electronic library from the standpoint of an individual subject discipline. The European Decomate II project is developing

> an end-user service which provides access to heterogeneous information resources over different libraries in Europe using

a uniform interface, leading to a working demonstrator of the European Digital Library for economics.[38]

A number of different types of information resource will be made available including library catalogues and other bibliographic databases, full text research papers, journal articles and theses, multimedia publications and Internet resources. One of the main project issues has been the question of what resources to include and what to omit. This issue has a number of dimensions including scholarly, technical and economic. In the mid to long term the economics of both institutional resource provision[39] and cooperative collection development are likely to be difficult to resolve.[40]

End-users, in contrast to the information providers, will no doubt expect the electronic resources and services to be available at all times and indefinitely. However, it may be that a complex provision and access model will have to be established to identify priorities of access within individual institutions, as it may not be possible to make all resources constantly available, and the needs of users will clearly change over time. Availability of any single resource or resource collection may depend upon timeliness, anticipated volume of use, the number of simultaneous users, licensing arrangement and so on. Local access policies may well be dictated and influenced by regional and national caching and mirroring initiatives. These will allow specifically selected resource collections to be made more accessible to those who will make use of them. Lancaster and Sandore say that:

> one can now visualise a library as providing various levels of access to electronic resources . . . Electronic resources in great demand (Level A) are made permanently accessible through a campus network, while others (level B) can be accessed remotely via the campus network when needed (e.g. through the Internet) . . . The library may have been responsible for selecting the level A resources from the international network and downloading them to the campus network. It may also have been responsible for building the indexes or providing the pointers that draw attention to level B resources. The level C and D resources are not available through the campus network but must be used within the library through a local area network or a single dedicated workstation.[41]

A further complication is the need to establish secure authentication and authorization procedures to ensure that only registered members of the institution are able to gain access to those resources where strict licence agreements are in force.[42]

Document delivery ▮

One of the main benefits of the electronic library will be the ability to deliver information services to the user's desktop to save the user going to the library at all. If material becomes available only electronically then users might just as well access the resources from their own desks rather than making the trip to the library. Some non-higher educational institutions have already developed extensive campus intranets with extensive course material, resulting in the replacement of most of the shelves of textbooks in the library with banks of PCs linked into the intranet and other electronic resources. The first project to build a working electronic library for use by students in a UK university was the ELINOR project which ran from 1992 to 1996 at De Montfort University. The main impetus was the likelihood that in the future not all sites would be able to keep sufficient printed copies of all books for all courses.

> ELINOR was a two phase pilot project with three overall goals: first to create a pilot system and, in so doing address some of the issues involved (technical, copyright, selection & acquisition of materials, and the user aspects); second, to investigate the expansion of a small-scale electronic library to a larger distributed library system; and third, as of necessity, to develop a more efficient and effective means of accessing and sharing resources within a networked multi-campus institution.[43]

A potential difficulty with regard to electronic journals is the choice of format for the storage and delivery of electronic journals. Until academics and students become accustomed to using e-journals, integrity of the journal look and layout may need to be retained. There are a number of different formats that might be used to retain the look and feel of a printed journal, none of which is yet a universal standard, although Adobe's PDF (Portable Document Format) is now widely used.[44] These all require additional software on the user's desktop to allow the format to be handled, which may hinder their acceptance. In the long term, developments such as Java should allow the electronic journal and the required viewing software to be delivered to the desktop simultaneously.

Publishers, publishing and publications ▮

One of the problems hindering many document delivery projects is the unwillingness of publishers to make material available for inclusion in digital collections, and this was keenly felt by the ELINOR project team.[45] Clearly publishers wish to protect their revenue and profits, but in the long term the electronic library will only be truly feasible if it provides at least the equivalent of the print-based library.[46] Derek Law, one of the pioneers of networked academic information in the UK, where the emphasis has been on making information access free at the point of use, has long recognized this as a problem. He said in 1992:

> worrying for the users is the concentration of publications in an even smaller number of multinational conglomerates [who] threaten to create a near monopoly on commercial information transfer. All too few academic authors realise how easily they sign away copyright to publishers, so they may not even copy their own material. The very notion of intellectual property becomes difficult when material is 'published' across networks.[47]

Libraries will have to continually assess their balance of printed versus electronic resources as the quantity of the former declines. This will have to be done in the context of the overall library materials budget and what electronic publications are available for purchase. Complex subscription models involving both printed and electronic resources, holdings versus access provision, coupled with flexible royalty and licensing arrangements are likely to be the norm for the foreseeable future, with pioneering libraries having little previous experience to call upon. The decision of Aston University in Birmingham (UK) to subscribe to the ADONIS document delivery service in 1992 allowed them to gain access to 500 electronic journals but at the loss of printed journals. However, at the time their ADONIS supplier did not envisage the system being used as a replacement for printed subscriptions. The royalty payment system imposed for printing made financial planning difficult, especially as many of the extra journals were only peripheral to Aston's teaching and expected use could not easily be calculated.[48]

In addition to the creation of electronic versions of existing print journals, the electronic library will see the development of new hypermedia and multimedia-enhanced journals which can take full advantage of the new technologies and integrate scholarly writing with teaching and learning materials. A number of these were funded under the eLib programme.[49-52] The ease with which Web pages can be developed has encouraged a number of academics to create new Web journals which would otherwise not have been published. Academics may still be willing to use electronic journals only if they are published in parallel with printed versions, or the electronic journals are peer reviewed. In the early development of the electronic library, peer review will be an important consideration for both publishers and academics alike. Wilkinson suggests that:

> it could become even more important as electronic documents proliferate. In such an environment, peer review could help select credible items the reader wants from an overwhelming supply of information. But some researchers have suggested peer review is no longer needed and is simply an excuse for publishers to control information.[53]

In the long term a number of electronic resource items may not be published in the traditional sense, but only on demand, and supplied in a tailored form for individual users. Users may be able to pick and mix information content to retrieve a self-selected and created 'journal' issue. On demand publishing (ODP) will be a major area of development in the electronic library but is heavily dependent upon the stated needs of academics, researchers and students. However, instead of having to take out a subscription to fringe journals, or pay for whole printed journal issues, only those articles deemed to be of relevance to the courses being studied need be selected and paid for. The ERIMS (Electronic Readings in Management Studies: Templeton College, Oxford) eLib project has explored 'the longer term delivery of marked-up texts by working with selected academics authoring new texts.'[54] In addition to the question of what to make available is what the on-demand delivery time might be – will it be instantaneous or will there be some delay? A number of just-in-time electronic article delivery services have been established, many of them in the USA, which are investigating desktop journal provision on an 'as needed' basis.[55]

Not only will the content be held in one or more electronic format, but also the management of the resources will need to be electronic. Electronic administration systems will need to be developed which can handle such things as copyright clearance and royalty payments. The eLib project eOn focused on the establishment of a suitable model for ODP which incorporated cataloguing, copyright and charging mechanisms and which could be integrated into current educational provision.[56] There is no doubt that librarians need a better understanding of the economics of the electronic library, and models need to be developed which include appropriate pricing mechanisms for the supply and delivery for the whole range of information to be included. The European project Imprimatur is attempting to build a consensus about how intellectual property rights should be handled in the digital age.[57]

End-user training and awareness ■

The ability to use the electronic resources will be a key success factor. If users are unable to use the electronic resources or gain access to the resources to meet their need, then the electronic library will be considered a failure. In the long term, users will need to be trained to use the electronic library efficiently and effectively and be kept up to date with important changes to both content and interface. Anticipating the difficulties that many users would have using electronic and unfamiliar resources for the first time, a number of the eLib Access to Network Resources (ANR) projects were concerned with the creation of subject based information gateways designed for particular disciplines. One factor in promoting use was ensuring the quality of the selected resource links to demonstrate that they were a substantial improvement on what was generally on offer via the Internet. The designers of the engineering gateway Edinburgh Engineering Virtual Library (EEVL) made a point of informing users that their subject gateway was hand crafted and the resources selected by teams of experts.[58] However, this may not be enough for subject disciplines where the academics are not traditional computer users. The History Data Service (part of the UK's Arts and Humanities Data Service) identified a number of obstacles in attempting to get historians to exploit digital historical data.[59] These included:

- resistance within the historical community to the integration of computing into history
- lack of recognition for the research and scholarship involved in the creation and use of electronic resources for research and teaching
- insufficient resources and funding to provide historians with the means to successfully integrate electronic resources in their research and teaching
- lack of critical mass of quality resources
- lack of standards
- lack of a fully developed and consistent support hierarchy
- insufficient skills among the historical community to exploit the potential.

The role of librarian as trainer and educator can be crucial here, as discovered in the eLib TAPin (Training and Awareness Programme in networks) project based at University of Central England in Birmingham, where a model of training and awareness for academics was created and applied across different disciplines.[60]

Individual user needs ▮

Users of the electronic library will increasingly expect the provision of new services both for themselves and for their particular subject discipline. A major advantage that electronic resources have over printed materials is that they can be updated easily. However, the benefit may be lost if the user is unaware of changes made to resources since they were last used. A combination of alerting services or more recent developments such as push technology or intelligent agents will be required.[61] Users may also wish to handle the electronic information arriving at their desktop in a more personal way. One member of the ELINOR project team carried out some preliminary work on a prototype system called the Personal Digital Library (PDL) which:

> acts as a front-end to other electronic library systems and manages all the user's information needs. A PDL is intended to be an integrated information environment for the individual information user.

Essentially, it is a local, multi-view database of electronic documents and references, such as URLs (uniform resource locators), to other electronic library databases. The look and feel should be customizable, within the limits of the user's browser, but it should allow individuals to build up their own long-term personal resource collection or virtual library.[62] In the long term there is plenty of scope for enterprising libraries and/or companies to develop a range of packages designed to meet the specialized needs of electronic library users.

The hybrid library ▮

Although much of the current research is looking at the long-term implications of a fully functioning electronic library, in the short term it is likely that most educational libraries will be maintaining a mixture of both traditional printed resources and electronic resources. Several of the latest eLib projects (Phase 3) are exploring how best to blend this mixture where:

> the challenge now is to bring together technologies from these new developments, plus the electronic products and services already in libraries, and the historical functions of our local, physical libraries, into well organized, accessible hybrid libraries.[63]

This may require the institution to become more flexible to address the demands of the information age.[64] At the more technical level, the eLib project MODELS was 'motivated by the recognised need to develop an applications framework to manage the rapidly multiplying range of distributed heterogeneous information resources and services being offered to libraries and their users'. In particular it is seeking to exploit the issues involved in reducing the disjointedness between, what it refers to as, print and digital resource spaces.[65] The phrase 'information landscape' has been taken up by later hybrid library projects such as Agora (UKOLN) which believes that 'the library will continue to organise the assembly places where information users and information products are brought into useful contact.'[66] Rusbridge has written in detail about the contribution of the early eLib projects to the hybrid library,[67] but the latest projects should provide a better view on how best to manage them and organize the resource collections for the benefit of the end-users. HYLIFe is exploring the practicalities of delivering the mixture of print and electronic services required in future educational libraries with economical maintenance. The focus here is not technological, but on the needs of specific non-standard customers, and the required institutional, social and educational support. These customers include part-time students, remote users, practitioner/students and franchised colleges.[68] Malibu (King's College London) is developing appropriate management models for the hybrid library including the migration from current library structures to the new ones.[69] BUILDER (Birmingham University, UK) is developing a model of the hybrid library within both a teaching and research context. The project is investigating the use of metadata indexing for all resources including CAL packages. It is also exploring a number of teaching and learning issues such as integration of materials, support for teaching staff in the creation of intranet packages and the involvement of the university press in the publication and digitization of materials.[70,71]

Performance measurement

Some measurement of the performance of the electronic library will be crucial to determine its effectiveness, but what should be measured and how will it be achieved? Brophy and Wynne have drawn together the major contributions since 1990 to the development of library performance indicators, but have focused on the library manager's requirements which include not only information on evaluation and review but also operational management and forward

planning.[72] They have added a number of electronic library measures to the UK Joint Funding Council's Effective Academic Library
set of performance indicators but they have not been developed into
a single model. Young argues that the 'measurement of electronic
media and services presents significant challenges for libraries' and
requires a 'reconceptualization of library quantitative measures.'[73]
He advocates using a combination of different measures which are
based on transactions, time, cost and use. However, it will be difficult to measure the individual use made by users of their own personal information collections held at their desktop. Lancaster and
Sandore suggest that 'the most obvious evaluation criterion would
relate to the frequency with which an individual needs to go beyond
personal and institutional resources to satisfy a particular need.'[74]
However, it may yet be too early to develop an appropriate evaluation model, as user groups, information-seeking behaviour, the role
of the library, and available datasets will all change as the electronic
library begins to develop.

Conclusion

This chapter has explored a number of issues surrounding the introduction of the electronic library. However, the electronic library will
not be a once and for all creation and will need to evolve over time.
It is likely to form part of a much larger institutional information
management system possibly operating in an international context.
Recent and continuing research projects have been useful in identifying some of the key problems and obstacles to be faced on the way
to achieving institution-wide acceptance of the electronic library.
Much work remains to be done in many areas some of which have
not traditionally involved librarians, and some of which have yet to
be seriously addressed. These include:

- design of appropriate system integration and architecture
- potential scalability of electronic library models to different size
  institutions
- knowledge representation
- networked information tools and paradigms
- multilinguality
- economic and social implications
- handling of graphics, models and multimedia in a user-centred
  working environment
- adequate performance measurement tools.

Notes

1 F.W. Lancaster and B. Sandore (1997) *Technology and Management in Library and Information Services*. Champaign, IL: Graduate School of Library and Information Science, University of Illinois, p.84.

2 eLib Electronic Libraries: http://www.ukoln.ac.uk/services/elib/background/

3 Higher Education Funding Councils (1993) *Joint Funding Councils' Libraries Review Group: Report* (Follett Report). Bristol: HEFC, p.5. Also available at: http://www.ukoln.ac.uk/services/papers/follett/report/

4 C. Davies, M. Hall, C. Oppenheim and A. Scammell (1997) *Early Impact of eLib Activities on Cultural Change in Higher Education* (Electronic Libraries Programme Studies). London: Library Information Technology Centre. Also available at: http://www.ukoln.ac.uk/services/elib/papers/

5 *The eLib Phase 3 Programme: Hybrid Libraries and Large Scale Resource Discovery . . . and Digital Preservation*: http://www.ukoln.ac.uk/services/elib/background/pressreleases/summary2.html

6 B.J. Reid and W.T. Foster (eds) (2000) *Achieving Cultural Change in Networked Libraries*. London: Gower.

7 M. Brodie and N. McLean (1995) Process reengineering in academic libraries: shifting to client-centered resource provision, *CAUSE/EFFECT Magazine*, 18(2): 40–6. Also available in different formats from: http://www.educause.edu/pub/ce/cem95/cem952.html

8 Reference at note 5 above shows the original thinking on this concept. Volume 4 of *The New Review of Information and Library Research* is largely devoted to reports from the hybrid library projects funded by JISC.

9 R. Lloyd-Owen (1997) On-demand publishing – researching its application to some library problems: Project Phoenix. *Library & Information Briefings*, 74(August): 2–21.

10 J.E. Klobas (1997) Information services for the new millenium organizations: librarians and knowledge management, in D. Raitt (ed.) *Libraries for the New Millennium*. London: Library Association, pp.39–64.

11 Higher Education Funding Councils op. cit.

12 L. Watson (1998) Information services: a mission and a vision, *Ariadne*, 14(March): 6–7. Also available at http://www.ariadne.ac.uk/issue14/

13 W.H. Graves, C.G. Jenkins and A.S. Parker (1995) Development of an electronic information policy framework, *CAUSE/EFFECT Magazine*, 18(2): 15–23. Also available in different formats from: http://www.educause.edu/pub/ce/cem95/cem952.html

14 P. Brophy and P. Wynne (1997) *Management Information Systems and Performance Measurement for the Electronic Library (MIEL2)*, Electronic Libraries Programme Studies. London: Library Information Technology Centre, p.2.

15 N. McLean (1997) The global scholarly infrastructure: the quest for sustainable solutions. Paper to Beyond the beginning: the global scholarly information, an international conference organized by United Kingdom Office of Library Networking (UKOLN), Queen Elizabeth II Conference Centre, London, 16–17 June. Available from: http://www.ukoln.ac.uk/services/papers/bl/blri078/content/repor~10.htm

16 M. Collier (1998) A view from the hill, *Ariadne*, 14(March): 3. Also available at: http://www.ariadne.ac.uk/issue14/

17 C. Steele (1997) Managing change in digital structures, in D. Raitt (ed.) *Libraries for the New Millennium*. London: Library Association, pp.148–68.

18 B. Sloan (1997) *Service Perspectives for the Digital Library: Remote Reference Services*, http://alexia.lis.uiuc.edu/~sloan/e-ref.html

19 C. Bartle, J. Cade, S. Curry, A. Hutton and M. Jackson (1997) Organizational and cultural change in higher education LIS, *Information UK Outlooks*, 29(November).

20 B.A. Rapple (1997) The electronic library: new roles for librarians, *CAUSE/EFFECT Magazine*, 20(1): 45–51. Also available in different formats at: http://www.educause.edu/pub/ce/cem97/cem971.html

21 J. Day, G. Walton, M. Bent, S. Curry, C. Edwards and M. Jackson (1998) *The Impact on People of Electronic Libraries: Monitoring Organizational and Cultural Change in UK Higher Education*, http://ilm.unn.ac.uk/cni4.htm See also the main IMPEL site at http://ilm.unn.ac.uk/impel/

22 H. Geleijnse (1994) A library of the future, *Library Association Record*, 96(2): 10–11.

23 M.B. Fecko (1997) *Electronic Resources: Access and Issues*. London: Bowker Saur.

24 D. Nicholson and M. Smith (1998) Electronic resource creation and management at Scottish universities: survey results and demonstrator service progress, *Ariadne* 14(March): 9–10. Also available at: http://www.ariadne.ac.uk/issues14. See also the CATRIONA Web site at: http://catriona2.lib.strath.ac.uk/catriona/

25 M.W. Ghikas (1989) Collection management for the 21st century, *Journal of Library Administration*, 11(1/2): 123. Quoted in Lancaster and Sandore op. cit., p.88.

26 L. Carpenter, A. Prescott and S. Shaw (eds) (1998) *Towards the Digital Library: The British Library's Initiatives for Access Programme*. London: British Library.

27 Anon. (1996) Digital library development programme, *British Library Research and Innovation Centre Research Bulletin*, 15(Autumn): 1–2. Contact John Draper at john.draper@bl.uk

28 J. Plent (1998) Building the Distributed National Electronic Resource (DNER), *JISC News*, spring: 5.

29 D. Haynes, D. Streatfield, T. Jowett and M. Blake (1997) *Responsibility for Digital Archiving and Long Term Access to Digital Data*, Electronic Libraries Programme Studies. Archive, *D-Lib Magazine*. London: Library Information Technology Centre.

30 S.M. Griffin (1998) NSF/DARPA/NASA, *Digital Libraries*, July/August. Also available at: http://www.dlib.org/dlib/july98/07griffin.html

31 H.M. Gladney (1998) Safeguarding digital library contents and users, *D-Lib Magazine*, July/August. Also available at: http://www.dlib.org/dlib/july98/gladney/07gladney.html

32 P. Lyman and B. Kahle (1998) Archiving digital cultural artifacts: organizing an agenda for action, *D-Lib Magazine*, July/August. Also available at: http://www.dlib.org/dlib/july98/07lyman.html

33 N. Beagrie and D. Greenstein (1998) *Digital Collections: A Strategic Policy Framework for Creating and Preserving Digital Resources*, http://ahds.ac.uk/manage/framework.htm

34 Details of projects at: http://www.kcl.ac.uk/projects/srch/backgrd/guide/guideindex.htm

35 http://www.rslp.ac.uk

36 http://www.ukoln.ac.uk/services/elib/papers/other/anderson

37 (1998) Digimap.Plus Background to the Digimap.Plus project, http://digimap.ed.ac.uk:8081/project/digi_background.html

38 Decomate-II (1998) http://www.bib.uab.es/project/eng/d11.htm

39 F. Fishwick, L. Edwards and J. Blagden (1998) *Scholarly Electronic Journals: Economic Implications*, Electronic Libraries Programme Studies. London: Library Information Technology Centre.

40 E. Chapman (1998) Buying shares in libraries: the economics of cooperative collection development, *International Federation of Library Associations Journal*, 24(2): 102–6.

41 Lancaster and Sandore op. cit., p.143.

42 A. Glenn and D. Millman (1998) Access management of web-based services: an incremental approach to cross-organizational authentication and authorization, *D-Lib Magazine*, September. Also available at: http://www.dlib.org/dlib/September98/millman/09millman.html

43 A. Ramsden (ed.) (1998) *ELINOR: Electronic Library Project*. London: Bowker Saur, p.1.

44 H. Brailsford (1998) Parallel publishing and the scholarly journal, *Library & Information Briefings*, 82(May).

45 Ramsden op. cit.

46 C.J. Armstrong and R. Lonsdale (1998) *The Publishing of Electronic Scholarly Monographs and Textbooks*, Electronic Libraries Programme Studies. London: Library Information Technology Centre.

47 D. Law (1992) Can the virtual library become a reality?, *Computer Bulletin*, November/December: 2–3.

48 A. Cameron (1996) CD-ROM and document delivery, in R. Biddiscombe (ed.) *The End-User Revolution*. London: Library Association Publishing, pp.119–34.

49 *CLIC Consortium Electronic Journal Project:* http://www.ch.ic.ac.uk/clic/

50 *Internet Archaeology:* http://intarch.ac.uk/

51 *JILT: The Journal of Information, Law and Technology:* http://elj.warwick.ac.uk/

52 *Open Journal Framework:* http://journals.ecs.soton.ac.uk/

53 S.L. Wilkinson (1998) Electronic publishing takes journals into a new realm, *Chemical & Engineering News*, 18 May. Also available at: http://pubs.acs.org/hotartcl/cenear/980518/elec.html

54 ERIMS: http://www.templeton.ox.ac.uk/www/college/library/erims/intro.htm

55 High Wire Press Just-in-time(sm): electronic article delivery services: http://www.public.iastate.edu/~CYBERSTACKS/Just.htm

56 eOn: http://www.eon.uel.ac.uk/

57 Imprimatur (Intellectual Multimedia Property Rights Model And Terminology for Universal Reference): http://www.imprimatur.alcs.co.uk/

58 R. Macleod, L. Kerr and A. Guyon (1998) The EEVL approach to providing a subject based information gateway for engineers, *Program*, 32(3): 205–23. Web site can be seen at http://www.eevl.ac.uk/

59 History Data Service. Scholarly exploitation of digital resources: a workshop for historians: http://hds.essex.ac.uk/reports/user_needs/final_report01.stm

60 TAPin: http://www.uce.ac.uk/tapin/

61 A. Walker (1998) The Internet knowledge manager, dynamic digital libraries, and agents you can understand, *D-Lib Magazine*, March. Also available at: http://www.dlib.org/dlib/march98/walker/03walker.html

62 D. Zhao (1998) The personal digital library, in A. Ramsden (ed.) *ELINOR: Electronic Library Project*. London: Bowker Saur, p.97.

63 *The eLib Phase 3 Programme: Hybrid Libraries and Large Scale Resource Discovery . . . and Digital Preservation*: http://www.ukoln.ac.uk/services/elib/background/pressreleases/summary2.html

64 C. Field (1998) Building on shifting sands: information age organisations, *Ariadne*, 17(September). Also available at: http://www.ariadne.ac.uk/issue17/

65 *Models (Moving to Distributed Environments for Library Services). Models: overview*: http://www.ukoln.ac.uk/dlis/models/overview.html

66 Agora: http://hosted.ukoln.ac.uk/agora/scope.html

67 C. Rusbridge (1998) Towards the hybrid library, *D-Lib Magazine*, July/August. Also available at: http://mirrored.ukoln.ac.uk/lis-journals/dlib/dlib/dlib/july98/rusbridge/07rusbridge.html

68 HyLIFe (HYbrid LIbraries of the FuturE): http://www.unn.ac.uk/~xcu2/hylife/

69 Malibu (MAnaging the hybrid LIbrary for the Benefit of Users): http://www.kcl.ac.uk/humanities/cch/malibu/

70 BUILDER (Birmingham University Integrated Library Development and Electronic Resource): http://builder.bham.ac.uk/

71 S. Pinfield, J. Eaton, C. Edwards *et al.* (1998) Realizing the hybrid library, *D-Lib Magazine*, October. Available at: http://mirrored.ukoln.ac.uk/lis-journals/dlib/dlib/dlib/october98/10pinfield.html

72 Brophy and Wynne op. cit.

73 P. Young (1998) Measurement of electronic services in libraries: statistics for the digital age, *IFLA Journal*, 24(3): 158.

74 Lancaster and Sandore op. cit., p.223.

10

INFORMATION MANAGEMENT: FUTURE PERFECT OR PAST IMPERFECT?

Derek Law

By common consent we are entering the third great revolution of humankind, the information revolution. The UK prime minister, Tony Blair, is quoted in the preface to this volume as comparing the importance of the information revolution to that of the agricultural and industrial revolutions. That comparison is often made but it conceals an important truth. The key feature of the agricultural revolution was not the use of the plough to allow planting, but the development of wheeled carts which allowed the distribution of food and the development of trade. The key feature of the industrial revolution was not the invention of the steam engine, but the development of the network of canals and railways, which allowed the distribution of raw materials and finished products to allow economics to develop. In the same way the key feature of the information society is not the computer, but the development of networks which allow the global distribution of information. In every case development has sprung from the distribution mechanism.

Universities have always been international in their nature and ambitions and more recently further education colleges have developed international links. They also possess some of the most advanced networks in the world. Information is the foundation of education. As this book has shown, it permeates every aspect of university and college life and its creation, dissemination, understanding and preservation are what we all do. Yet the very fact that it is pervasive allows us to take it for granted and to ignore the threats to our traditional lifeblood. For the first time multinational corporations have begun to buy up information while several companies, for example Motorola, Ford, British Aerospace, have begun to explore setting up 'universities'. At the same time we continue to allow staff to hand over all rights in the information we create. European legislation which protects the rights-holders rather than users is growing and many practices we have taken for granted about the use of information are being eroded.

There is an interesting analogy with the privatization of the UK water companies. Like information, water was and is an essential commodity that was taken for granted and, if not free, was so cheap that it might have been. Then came privatization. Prices rose dramatically; users were cut off for non-payment. Supplies dried up through a mixture of incompetence and underinvestment; private profit replaced public good in all sorts of environmental areas; rivers were sucked dry; the fact that the water companies were now in the private sector meant that the government found itself almost powerless to intervene. The comparison with the increasingly aggressive private information sector is all too obvious.

Some institutional leaders also adopt a dangerously complacent attitude, assuming that the Internet will somehow provide ready access to information. They run the risk of forgetting that education is at least as much a producer of information as a consumer and that the creation of a teaching or research model which relies on students behaving like mouse potatoes concedes the battle to our emerging competitors. This is all the more ironic since the Internet as it is at present is almost wholly inimical to academic pursuits.

Internet meltdown?

A whole host of problems surround the electronic equivalent of bibliographic control. Some are a function of the medium while others are variations of old issues. A thread which runs through all of the problems is the failure of the academy to recognize that the problems exist. The Internet is seen as a great and liberating development, but it is not a neutral development and requires very substantial international effort if it is to be made usable for sustained scholarly communication rather than short-term gratification. The problems begin at the most basic levels.

The very act of naming and identifying electronic objects consistently is fraught with difficulty. A book or a filed letter is a static object which does not change over time. In an electronic environment there is a need to reference objects as they move and change over time and place. The temporary nature of URLs is notorious and it has been claimed that they have an average life of 75 days. Even where the URL remains constant, issues of version control and quality assurance remain unresolved. The seriousness of this problem cannot be overemphasized, for the continuity of citation is central to scholarship and without it scholarship cannot flourish. Some attempts are being made to deal with this problem, the current favourite being digital object identifiers. These originate from the commercial publishing world and it is not then clear whether they have validity and applicability beyond the commercial sector. A significant if unquantified proportion of the material held in any organization and in any medium is either non-commercial or out of copyright and any new system must be able to embrace everything from incunables to examination papers.

The issue of naming objects is also difficult and as yet unresolved. At present anyone can name an object with no obligation to maintain names over time. This is compounded by the fact that many of the reference points we take for granted in the print world disappear. A book published by Oxford University Press implies a set of values, standards and scholarly rigour that is understood. But an address incorporating the phrase 'ox.ac.uk' could be anything from a university press to a student PC in a rented room. The persistence of object names is a long way from having a settled structure – and there is little evidence that the official bodies in scholarship understand the threat this poses.

Metadata and the description of objects is in rather better case. The Dublin Core standard first produced by Stu Weibel at OCLC (Online Computer Library Centre) has very rapidly developed international acceptance with participation in standards work from Europe, USA and the Pacific Rim. But even here much work remains to be done. Cataloguing has historically described static and largely immutable objects. The Internet offers new genres of multimedia and even services which will require appropriate description. This work remains to be developed.

Unlike the book, terms and conditions of use must also be described for electronic materials. Many will have multiple copyright permissions, many will be licensed rather than purchased, many will have restrictions on categories of users – and these will vary according to the terms of sale rather than be inherent in the product. Although the initial success of the Dublin Core gives confidence that these problems can be resolved, a great deal of international effort will be required to create a usable system.

Searching and indexing have proved much more difficult technically than the designers of Web robots would have us believe. Web indexing systems are breaking down as their architecture collapses under the weight of data. It is increasingly common to undertake a search on Lycos or Excite or Infoseek and recover hundreds of thousands of hits in apparently random order. Much work is going on here but designers despair at the inability or unwillingness of the public to master Boolean searching and most systems still have a long way to go to beat a half-way competent reference librarian. Web searching has undoubtedly transformed the ability of searchers to acquire a whole range of current reference information, but is dramatically poor at discovering scholarship and research.

Unlike the print world, the electronic one will require validation of the rights of the user. User authentication is regarded as an essential element of electronic commerce, but it too lacks basic elements for the furtherance of scholarly activity. At present there are no good ways of proving membership of the 'data club' when away from the parent institution. Scholars visiting another institution, students on vacation or researchers on field trips are difficult to validate. There is then a very knotty problem surrounding usage data. On the one hand commercial publishers wish to collect usage information as a marketing tool. They are, however, unwilling to release this information to libraries so that they can judge whether usage justifies subscription. On the other hand many users do not wish anyone to know what they are reading or researching. Traditionally, organizations have preserved the anonymity of user data except where criminal acts are suspected. Is this a right or simply a custom?

Then there are a series of issues and old battlegrounds to revisit. Rights management systems are growing quickly and are promoted largely by commercial concerns. They provide many areas of philosophic contention. As mentioned above, the question of whether the user can remain anonymous conflicts with commercial need. The issue of preservation remains technically, legally and operationally unresolved. Historically this has been the domain of the national libraries for published information and of the originating organizations for their own archives, but it is not clear that they will or can perform the same role in an electronic environment. We cannot reasonably expect preservation to be undertaken by publishers. Furthermore, the whole issue of fair use is being revisited by publishers, some of whom declare that it does not or cannot exist electronically. Major battles need to be undertaken on these issues, again with little evidence that the academy understands or cares about the issues.

The preservation and archiving of electronic information has barely surfaced as a very complex issue. The Data Archive at the University of Essex has existed since 1967 and has perhaps as clear a picture as anywhere of the so far intractable problems of storing, refreshing and kitemarking information. The problems are staggeringly complex technically and staggeringly expensive to resolve. Although some progress is being made on the legal deposit of commercial material, little appears to be done on the non-commercial and primary materials of scholarship. There are no standards or control or approval mechanisms for institutions or data repositories. This position may be compared with that in the United Kingdom where archives are expected to meet the BS5454 standard and the Historical Manuscripts Commission takes an active interest in the state of repositories and where archivists have specialist professional training. A new class of electronic material, what Clifford Lynch of CNI (Coalition for Networked Information) has called 'endangered content', is emerging, where the formal and informal records of disciplines are effectively at risk through neglect.[1] Archives collect papers, but institutions do not sample or preserve the email or word-processed files of their scholars. Lab books are routinely preserved by scientists but it is doubtful if any institution has a policy for the preservation of digitally captured images or data from research equipment.

Network topology is barely discussed as an issue due to a naive assumption that there will be an infinitely expanding amount of bandwidth which will somehow be made available to scholarship. And yet there is no evidence to support this view. US universities have abandoned the failing Internet provided by telecommunications companies to create Internet II as a private network attuned to their needs. In Europe the relatively modest ambition of the European Union to link existing research networks through the TEN-34 Project has been 'shaped by a series of non-technical influences such as non-availability of required public services',[2] while 'standard PNO (public network operator) services in Europe could not fulfil the requirements of the R&D community in Europe'.[3] Equally the assumption that we accept a simple commercial approach to network planning is questionable. At present in the UK, bandwidth is acquired in the light of use rather than as a result of scholarly or educational policy decisions. Thus bandwidth expands at a great rate to the east coast of North America to meet traffic growth. There is almost no debate on whether policy should drive such acquisition and route bandwidth say to southern Africa then India, Singapore, Australia and then the west coast of the USA opening up markets and scholarship to what is sometimes called UK Higher Education Limited. There is a creeping form of cybercolonialism in the assumption that only the USA has digital material of value to the world. It is interesting to note the recent decision of the Australian vice-chancellors to use network charges to discriminate against overseas

Web sites and in favour of Australian ones.[4] No discussion appears to take place of how the products and output of small learned societies are to be mirrored around the world and what standards and quality controls will apply to mirror sites. Again the scholarly community is silent while the commercial giants of the STM world dictate the shape of electronic scholarly communication – despite the fact that large scientific publishers are aberrant rather than the norm.

Nor is the network yet totally robust. A Dilbert cartoon pointedly and uncomfortably accurately suggested that all of the time saved through automation in the information age had been lost by people sitting at Web browsers waiting for pages to load. Networks do not yet for example give the reliable quality of service required for multicasting, while video clips have all the power, quality and assurance of early silent films. It should be self-evident that for research institutions working at the leading edge of scholarship and indeed telecommunications, the standard services provided by Internet service providers will always be inadequate.

A more positive element which is emerging in the electronic era is the broadening of what constitutes content. Services such as the Arts and Humanities Data Service,[5] based at King's College London, or the excellent SCRAN (Scottish Cultural Resources Access Network) project,[6] funded by the museums of Scotland, are much involved in the digitization of museum and archive collections. This is happening fast and brings relevant experience in activities such as new licensing models and standards. It also highlights the role of curators in the digital environment as relating to presentation as well as preservation. But again there appears to be little concerted effort by the official organs of scholarship to build formal cross-domain linkages.

It is increasingly appropriate to question whether the Internet is the most appropriate general vehicle for information provision. This is a recognition that unrestricted international access is not a good use of resources and that a combination of local resources, mirror sites and caches can be more effective.

The Internet is wonderful when it works, but for large numbers of resources it is almost unusable. Very little thought has been given to alternative models in the rush to connect to what is good. The irony in this is that we have an excellent model for an alternative strategy in the classic library. It is a paradox of networks that electronic resources may make it worth reconsidering returning to a holdings strategy rather than an access strategy for information. As the cost of filestore drops and becomes competitive with bandwidth costs, it may be proper to acquire and hold information locally.

What then are the main messages from this book?

- The time is ripe for colleges and universities to play an increasingly significant role in the learning age, in lifelong learning, in the local, regional and national political, cultural and economic agenda.
- Effective and efficient management of information and the move towards knowledge-based approaches will be crucial for further and higher education to manage within a context of change and growth and to contribute fully to networked learning opportunities.
- Mature information strategies, which consider the whole way in which information is created, purchased, accessed, managed, exploited and disposed of within individual institutions, allied to the individual culture, the way people work and questions of ownership of information are fundamental to future effective growth and development in further and higher education.
- Countries throughout the world are trying to transform themselves into information societies; societies that can grow and prosper through the more effective use of information and its associated technologies. But we must recognize that the technology of global communication brings with it a considerable threat to national and local cultures. There is danger that the distinctive European culture, in all its richness and diversity, will become smothered by a bland global culture, manufactured in Hollywood and deigned to meet the desires of the majority.
- There is a real danger that the information society will reinforce and deepen social exclusion rather than help to overcome it. We already have a European society in which the minority are excluded from the mainstream of social benefit through poor education, lack of employment, low incomes, disability and poor housing. We need to ensure that the creation of an information society does not exclude them further.
- Easy access to information, as a result of improved availability to IT in colleges and universities, has increased the expectation of the internal customer so that administrators have had to make more and more internal and external management information available to all. This has enabled responsive, devolved management and administration, the delegation of information ownership and the increasing use of more flexible working patterns. The role of the administrator is changing towards one of partnership with the 'customers', adding value through provision of the highest quality information and data together with analysis and commentary providing the tools and infrastructure to access appropriate information in a timely way.

- Information overload needs to be countered by the development of criteria that differentiate good and poor quality information.
- ICT offers great possibilities for making information seeking more comprehensive and richer, presenting results in motivating and informative ways, making research more democratic and pointing the way to more effective information seeking; however, information stress, over hasty abandonment of traditional libraries and an erosion of quality of information may counteract the benefits.
- A number of different technologies have a place in the learning cycle and each can add value to the students' learning experience but face-to-face communication and traditional teaching methods should not be forgotten; a balanced, managed approach is necessary to ensure quality of learning.
- Intellectual property issues need to be adequately understood and addressed in both print and other media forms and the knowledge base preserved.
- The UK government's lifelong learning agenda will require more 'joined-up' thinking, particularly with regard to library and information resources and the need for collaborative solutions to cross-sectoral use of libraries.

But above all perhaps the message of all the authors is that although information is a staple of educational life, it is one whose taste and flavour can be improved with consistent care and attention.

Notes ▪

1 Discussed in an unpublished paper given at the European Union Telematics Conference in Barcelona, February 1998.
2 M. Behringer (1997) The implementation of TEN-34. Paper presented at JENC8, the eighth annual Joint European Networking Conference, May, and later published in DANTE IN PRINT, 28, at: http://www.dante.net/pubs/dip/28/28html
3 Ibid.
4 News report in *The Times Higher* 1322, 6 March 1998.
5 http://www.ahds.ac.uk/
6 http://www.scran.ac.uk/

INDEX

HIGHER EDUCATION AND THE LAW
A GUIDE FOR MANAGERS

David Palfreyman and David Warner (eds)

Higher education is now 'big business' and a complex business. Increasingly, students demand value for money and are willing to resort to law if they feel they are not getting a fair deal and their complaints are being ignored. At the same time, higher education managers must keep abreast of legislation and become involved in ever more detailed contractual arrangements in matters such as mergers, franchising, property management and income generation.

The twenty-one chapters of this book give a comprehensive coverage of the issues and are contributed by law firms based in London, Birmingham, Oxford and Cambridge which all have substantial experience of advising higher education clients. This guide has been written for the non-lawyer, for the busy manager seeking guidance on potential legal problems and looking to avoid them by means of a preventive legal health check. It will help ensure value for money from solicitors by helping higher education institutions to be better informed and legally aware clients.

Contents
Part 1: Contexts – Setting the scene – What is higher education institution as a legal entity? – Part 2: Governance – Governance in an era of accountability and potential personal liability – Charity trusteeship: unlimited personal liability, again? – The law of meetings – Part 3: The higher education institution and its staff and students – The higher education institution – student contract – The regulation of the community: Student discipline, staff discipline, grievances and harassment codes – Disputes I: the role of the visitor in the chartered institutions – Disputes II: the scope for judicial review in the statutory institutions – Part 4: The higher education institution and its academic activity – Intellectual property, copyright and trade-marks – The internet: a modern Pandora's box – Part 5: The higher education institutions as a business – Trading companies – Mergers and acquisitions – Franchising – The private finance initiative – The legal status of the students' union – Part 6: The higher education institution and its property – Security: surveillance, trespass, 'reasonable force' and 'clamping' – Houses in multiple occupation and what is a 'house'? – The implications for higher education institutions of the disability discrimination act 1995 – Part 7: Consequences – A guide to litigation – The impact to European law – Case list – Bibliography – A bibliographical essay on the visitor – A note on the universities and colleges education law network – Contact address for contributors – Index.

Contributors
The law firms which contribute to this book are as follows:
Travers Smith Braithwaite, Cole & Cole, Eversheds, Martineau Johnson, Linnels, Manches & Co., Mills & Reeve, Shakespeares.

384pp   0 335 19876 7   (Hardback)

HIGHER EDUCATION MANAGEMENT
THE KEY ELEMENTS

David Warner and David Palfreyman (eds)

Many higher education institutions are like small towns, meeting the needs of their members by providing not only specialist teaching and research activities but also residential accommodation, catering, telecommunications, counselling, sports facilities and so on. The management of these institutions is very complex, requiring both generalist and specialist knowledge and skills; and the move to formal strategic planning means that it is no longer acceptable for higher education managers to be aware only of their own relatively narrow areas of expertise. All new managers would benefit from an holistic perspective on managing a whole institution. As such individuals are promoted, such 'helicopter vision' becomes a precondition of their and their institution's success. *Higher Education Management* provides:

- the first comprehensive account of non-academic higher education management;
- contributions from distinguished practitioners of university management;
- a key resource for all aspiring, trainee and practising managers in higher education.

Contents
Setting the scene – Organizational culture – Strategic planning – Sources of funds and resource allocation – Financial management – Decision-making and committees – Personnel management – Student management – Postgraduate and research organization and management – Estate management – Campus support services – Student support services – External relations – Academic support services – Management student learning – Notes on the legal framework within which HEIs operate – Notes on further reading – Bibliography – Index.

Contributors
David Adamson, Frank Albrighton, Barry Benjamin, Mark Clark, Sue Dopson, Diana Eastcott, Bob Farmer, John Gledhill, Alison Hall, Colin Harrison, John Hogan, Ian McNay, David Palfreyman, Derek Philips, Russell Rowley, John Sandbach, Paddy Stephenson, Harold Thomas, Julia Thomas, David Warner.

256pp   0 335 19569 5   (Paperback)   0 335 19570 9   (Hardback)